Silenced

Discovering My Voice Within Life's Valleys

Tabitha Crusoe

WESTBOW
P R E S S®
A DIVISION OF THOMAS NELSON
& ZONDERVAN

THE HOLY BIBLE, NEW INTERNATIONAL VERSION®,
NIV® Copyright © 1973, 1978, 1984, 2011 by Biblica, Inc.®
Used by permission. All rights reserved worldwide.

This book is a work of non-fiction. Unless otherwise noted, the author
and the publisher make no explicit guarantees as to the accuracy of
the information contained in this book and in some cases, names
of people and places have been altered to protect their privacy.

WestBow Press books may be ordered through booksellers or by contacting:

WestBow Press
A Division of Thomas Nelson & Zondervan
1663 Liberty Drive
Bloomington, IN 47403
www.westbowpress.com
1 (866) 928-1240

Because of the dynamic nature of the Internet, any web addresses or
links contained in this book may have changed since publication and may
no longer be valid. The views expressed in this work are solely those
of the author and do not necessarily reflect the views of the publisher,
and the publisher hereby disclaims any responsibility for them.

Any people depicted in stock imagery provided by Thinkstock are
models, and such images are being used for illustrative purposes only.
Certain stock imagery © Thinkstock.

ISBN: 978-1-5127-7440-5 (sc)
ISBN: 978-1-5127-7442-9 (hc)
ISBN: 978-1-5127-7441-2 (e)

Library of Congress Control Number: 2017901756

Print information available on the last page.

WestBow Press rev. date: 2/15/2017

To my covenant marriage partner, my husband. This work would not have been written without his support, love, and encouragement. He shows a love for me every single day that truly reflects Christ's love for the church. I love you, babe!

Contents

Introduction

My husband and I were on a plane, heading out of East Asia to renew our visas when he leaned over to me and told me to watch the movie that the plane was showing. I was in my own world, listening to some praise music when he got my attention. Interested, I turned off my music and switched my headset cord over to the audio input for the movie. I learned it was a movie titled *The Book Thief*, a book that was later made into film. The story was set during the Second World War and focused on a young girl named Liesel who was placed with a foster family. I do not want to give away too much of the story, but I do want to share how God spoke clearly to me through one of the scenes in the movie. At the beginning of the movie, it becomes quickly apparent that she has a love for books. Later on, this young girl is encouraged by an influential character in the film to write her very own story. As she was being challenged to write, the Lord used those same scenes to speak to me and stir up a desire that he had already placed deep within me. God was speaking loudly and clearly to me with instructions for me to write. As that new dream was revealed in my heart, it would take another few weeks to understand what he wanted me to write about. He faithfully showed me that he wanted me to write about my life. Though I argued with him that it was not necessary to publish another book that told people about one's history—I was sure there were countless books in that genre—God continued to press on me to write my own autobiography.

I thought over and over on these instructions from the Lord and soon was able to visualize myself writing, but as I agreed to write, I still had no idea about the direction of the book. God kept that part to himself, and so I began writing this book you are reading in faith that he would lead me as I move forward. From the time the Lord called me to put my story on these pages till the conclusion of the first draft, I found a year had gone by almost exactly to the date of him telling me to write. Of course, that delighted me and encouraged me that the Lord was indeed helping me and leading me as I went.

During the course of the year I spent writing, an intense season of winter rolled into my life. This season was not a surprise to God, though it was for me. He knew it was coming, and he wanted me to continue writing and journaling while I went through it. However, in the midst of the storm, I had no clue what was going on, and for a few months, I could not bring myself to write because I was having so much difficulty. Yet as the stormy winter season was coming to its close, I was able to pick my pen up again and finish writing, but with a greater understanding of why the Lord had told me to write this book in the first place. With direction for the book and a passion to bring it to completion, I was able to finish. As you read through the chapters, you will notice a journal entry placed between each chapter. These journal entries will help you follow me into the winter season I experienced and onto God's purposes of that intense season. The chapters take you through my life up until now and eventually give you further insight into the journals I wrote. Each journal entry that I have included for the reader is real and raw with emotion. I allowed myself to be extremely vulnerable as I put these private thoughts, feelings, and times of processing within this book.

With all this said, I now invite you to look into my life and hopefully learn from my experiences from a child to adulthood, serving as a missionary on the field and returning home during an unexpected season and learning of a deeper calling from the Lord. My desire is for the reader to be inspired, encouraged, and again find hope to pursue the dreams placed deep within our hearts. My hope and prayer is that the Lord will use my struggles to encourage others so that those who are dealing through their own conflicts will believe that the Lord indeed uses storms in our lives to write our beautiful stories.

Chapter 1

A Story Forms

I vividly remember the day my mother, in response to my question of when my father was going to pick me up for the weekend, answered me abruptly with little concern in her voice that he would not be coming to get me, and she told me not to ask about him anymore. My guess at that time was correct. My biological father had walked out of my life yet again, and this time for good. Just two and a half years prior to that conversation with my mother, I was introduced to a man I greatly resembled in appearance. I was seven years old at the time, and I thought that my stepfather, whom I had previously thought was my father, was a great dad to have. So why did I need another one? It was confusing at first, and learning my real family name took time to get used to. But soon I learned that in my heart I had enough love for both of my fathers. So the day that my biological father did not show for my usual weekend visit with him and his family, I was heartbroken. I cried myself to sleep that night, but I did so silently so I would not bother my family with my disappointment—and because I took to heart my mother's instructions not to mention my real father again. Because I dealt with this alone, I assumed I was the reason my father did not return for me. At a very young age, I felt deep shame and rejection coupled with mourning from his absence in my life. But in the midst of my private suffering, I would soon meet God, my heavenly Father.

My mother had decided one day to search for a good church for us to attend. Prior to her making this decision, I thought church was a once-a-year event during the Easter holiday. I was ten years old when we started attending a church located in a suburb of Phoenix, Arizona, and I was so excited to learn that you could visit church once a week instead of only once a year. I remember the pastor being funny, and I remember he made an open invitation to accept Jesus by walking down the aisle to the front of the church. So I looked up at my mother and told her I wanted to accept Jesus. She said I could go down the aisle, and so I did just that. It was a big church for us. No, make that an *enormous* church. We had been to a much smaller one once before in another town we used to live in, and we had also attended my great-grandfather's church. He pastored in an even smaller church and in an even smaller town. Both visits were during the Easter celebration. (Believe me—I had a hard time understanding why they would build these nice buildings only to be used once a year!)

As I made my way slowly toward the front of this ginormous church with so many adults worshipping in it, I finally found myself standing in the front row. I stood there courageously along with the other strangers who were already standing there, and I closed my eyes and silently told God I believed in him. Then I turned right around and walked back toward my mother. My stepfather had not yet felt a need to attend church with my two half sisters, my mother, and me. After I made my way to them, I thought it was funny that my mother asked me with whom I had prayed. That is how big this new church was for us. After all, my mother had a hard time seeing where I had gone and with whom I had talked. I told her I just prayed to God and that no one had talked with me. I guess the deacons were not looking for a small ten-year-old girl walking down the aisle, and so I was overlooked. But in his grace and mercy, God did not overlook me, and he did indeed see me and hear my decision that morning. My mother smiled and said that the next week she would go with me down the aisle so that I could properly pray with someone about my decision. That just gave her an opportunity to rededicate her life to Christ, and it gave me an opportunity to give my testimony to someone for the first time about the decision I had made a week before.

Life immediately took on a new meaning and purpose. All those childlike questions I had always pondered were now simply answered with a trust that God was in control and that he would surely help me with those answers. One of the questions I had was in understanding my identity. Since my biological father refused to accept me as his daughter, I would simply find my identity in being God's child. My stepfather had fully accepted me as his daughter from the day he married my mother, but the events of learning at the age of seven that he was not my biological father created a silent rift between my family and me. My half sisters knew their father and had a relationship with him, and I was constantly reminded each time I spoke, read, or heard my last name that I belonged to someone who had rejected me. My stepfather could not officially adopt me for reasons a ten-year-old would not be able to understand, but that did not keep me from pleading with him to change my family name to his more than once. I felt like the family appendage—like a part that did not really fit in. Of course, these were just feelings and not how I was viewed by them, but it still was a lonely and confusing time for me. These emotions soon became the springboard that catapulted me into being hungry for a deep relationship with God.

Journal Entry

East Asia
January 30, 2014

Why do I have feelings of guilt for wanting to take time to reflect on my calling? Why do I believe this is all there is for me in this life as if I have arrived to all God has for me? What are these lies I believe? I've been thinking a lot on these negative emotions, and I have been pondering their roots. My first guess about the root emotion is that it comes from my feelings of unworthiness, which keep me from moving forward. My past, my mistakes, and the continuous battles with my parents to move forward in life have left me feeling defeated and unworthy. I must recognize that these lies— lies that I will not succeed in my calling, that I can't do it, that I'm not capable, and that my past mistakes have made me unworthy—are all an attempt by the enemy to hold me in bondage. This is *not* God's plan for me.

When did I give up? When did I lose my passion for life? When did I lose confidence in seeking to be all that he has created me to be? My ignorance has led me to this horrible captivity, and the sins of my parents and the constant overshadowing of my mother have discouraged me. The enemy's voice in my head needs to be silenced, and the voice of God needs to grow. Heal my spiritual ears, oh God. Speak into me as one encouraging a tiny flower to bloom again in its second spring season. I forgive my parents. I know they have not intentionally discouraged me, and their mistakes have not been made to intentionally harm me. Lord, I need self-esteem and confidence in you. I have been lacking in that my entire life. I have been clever to fake confidence, but inside I am utterly lacking. I project courage, but inside I am afraid. Lord, change this in me. It requires confidence and courage in you to move forward in my calling.

Chapter 2

My Encounter with a Living God

When I was twelve years old, my mother drove me, my half sisters, and our girlfriends to hear a children's evangelist on a Friday evening at our church. I had invited my friends to come to the special event so that they could learn about who Jesus was. I was confident that they, too, would be delighted to learn that they could know God.

As the evangelist was teaching about Jesus and his acceptance of little children, I listened intently to every word. The man had a talent for speaking on a child's level, and he made the gospel simple and clear that night. His call to the altar was also simple. He encouragingly said, "Little children, come to Jesus. Jesus is calling all the little children to himself. Come, come." Immediately after that compelling altar call, my thoughts were conflicted for a moment. I felt an urging by the Spirit to answer that call, but I thought to myself that I had already walked the aisle once before when I was ten years old.

The Spirit continued to speak loud and clear, and I did the only thing I knew to do. I left the pew, and with tears welling up in my eyes, I went straight down front. What I did not know at the time was that I had a following behind me. All of my friends and my family went to the altar as well. The deacons and church leaders then escorted all of us to the traditional counseling room to engage each of us with questions about our decisions to follow Christ. Because at this point I had already begun crying and shaking, my mother was holding me. I heard the church leader ask me questions, but I literally could not speak to answer him. All I did was cry and shake.

He was persistent though, and he talked with my mother while he waited for me to calm down, which never happened. Perhaps he knew what was taking place with me, or perhaps he was confused. My crying continued for a while, and this sweet church leader finally just decided to pray with my mother and me to rededicate my life back to Christ. I later found it odd to share with others that after receiving Christ at ten years old, I was already backsliding at twelve years old and in need of rededicating my *tumultuous* life back to Christ. It makes me smile today to remember how those around me had no idea that God was just simply giving me an outpouring of his Spirit to prepare me to serve him later on. That Friday evangelical event was my Pentecost experience, a powerful outpouring of God's Spirit. It was God responding to my hunger to know him more, and it still is a night I will never forget.

In that outpouring experience, I was fully aware of my sinful nature, as God's presence was heavy upon me. My tears were tears of repentance, and my shaking was the result of the power of the Holy Spirit. At that time in my walk with God, I had yet to read or even hear about Pentecost in the book of Acts along with all the other miracles that took place in the first churches of the New Testament. Looking around at the other children in the counseling room, I noticed how they appeared much more emotionless in their responses. Here I was receiving a heavy outpouring of the Holy Spirit in a very conservative church, a baptism nonetheless, and thus, I began a journey in my life that would later become my cross to carry.

Journal Entry

East Asia
February 1, 2014

I see a tree. The tree will eventually be cut down and carved into a beautiful wood carving. But right now all I have is a tree. There are no illustrations to work off from or any plans. This tree represents my destiny of how my life message will glorify God. All I have been shown is that there is a deeper call within a call. Jesus has revealed to me only this much. I don't have specifics yet or plans but a promise that a beautiful wood carving will be made. As I wait on the Lord for instructions, for a plan, an illustration to work from, I will hold onto his promise by faith and trust in him. Everything inside of me screams there is more to my life! I am at the beginning stages of a new phase that he wants to do through and in me. It is good to dream again!

Chapter 3

Growing Pains

My relationship with God was real prior to my Holy Spirit experience; however, after this outpouring, my relationship with him ventured down a path that was all too new and exciting for me. Overnight I grew in boldness with sharing my faith while my understanding of Scripture was becoming more evident. My new passion in life was to know God. What was unclear to me at the time, however, was the treacherous terrain this new path with God would take me. My love for Scripture led me to Paul's letter to the Philippians. Specifically, Philippians 3:7–11 (NIV) had become the passage I chose as my life theme. I love reading that passage, meditating on each word and longing to make it my own life passion to live out its truth. "I want to know Christ and the power of his resurrection and the fellowship of sharing in his sufferings, becoming like him in his death, and so, somehow, to attain to the resurrection from the dead." Embracing these powerful words at such a young age would be the start of a journey during which I would learn to die to self.

Junior high included my least favorite years of my education. In those years I sadly discovered how children follow the taught example of their peers and our culture by classifying one another based on the wealth of their family. I will never forget my sister naively asking my mother and stepfather which class we belonged in. She asked if we were first class, middle class, or of the poorer class. My mother replied that we were none of those. Amused, she explained that we were in the class between the middle and the poor. My sister became visibly upset with this answer, and she proclaimed that she was sure we were in the rich class. Although we did not have much in possessions and my sisters and I shared our clothes, toys, and one room with one another, we did have love in our family. That made us wealthier than most families that had multiple cars and televisions yet did not have love. The children at school, however, did not understand this. Attending class while learning to ignore the ugly remarks of students—all because of a lack of name brands on my attire—was becoming very normal. Even more upsetting, though, was living this nightmare on Sunday mornings as students in the church youth group who were suppose to be different treated us the same way. Our culture has bred into our children a backwardness of priorities, and money has become a god to many now.

I had no idea at the time though that one of my very good school girl friends recognized my unusual joy and happiness in life despite my few possessions. She grew jealous of my contentment and began comparing her life with mine. Whenever I would stay the night in her home, her mother, who was a single parent, treated me with adoration because of my happy attitude and how I respected my elders. My friend grew bitter toward me because she was unable to see the love her mother had for her. All she could see was the attention I would receive when I came to play. We had just begun our first year in middle school together, and in that year my friend had managed to convince two other dear friends of ours that I was a horrible friend. One day at school, these friends began to give me the cold shoulder. I was confused and deeply upset. Days later they told me that I was a terrible friend, and they began leaving hate notes in my school locker. By the end of that school year, my bullies had multiplied, and no one would speak to me. My first year in middle school had been a painful and confusing experience that broke my spirit and damaged my fun personality and confidence. And these were the same three friends I had invited with me to hear the evangelist preacher speak at that divine Friday children's event.

However, my second year of middle school brought me new friends, and with God's grace on me, I selected these friends carefully. I purposely found those that were treated as outcasts like me and befriended them. My sister was concerned with our family's social class at the time, and I was concerned with just surviving school each day, hoping no one noticed how my shoes never matched my outfit.

By the time I finished high school, God had taken my broken spirit and built in me a heart that was beginning to become more desperate for him. He used my school years to teach me compassion toward others and to engrain in me the understanding of the need for God's love in the lives around me. He had put a desire in me to one day venture to other nations that have not yet heard of his love for them. He taught me to build my confidence on being his child, not on what I had or did not have. He showed me my love of teaching Scripture and making it simple for others to understand. He strengthened me through my sufferings to prepare me for more difficult suffering to come.

Tabitha Crusoe

Journal Entry

East Asia
February 6, 2014

Last night, I was talking with my husband, which opened more of a conversation than I had intended. I shared with him how because of having to submit to our authority, the organization that sent us out as missionaries, I was feeling shame and guilt about being who God had created me to be. Our organization has its own culture that I feel I can never fully fit into. It also frowns upon women who have performed outside of the roles assigned them. I poured my heart out to Jordan, not knowing this was God's intention, and I shared my private battle as a square peg that was having difficulty fitting into a circle hole. I shared how I felt that because of the spiritual gifts God had given me (speaking in tongues, having dreams and visions, hearing angels speak to me, being able to prophesy, having faith for healing, and having a huge desire to preach God's Word), I would never be fully accepted or be given the freedom to walk and teach on these gifts.

Because of all of this, I felt I had been caged—caged for more than four years, prevented from being who God had created me to be! Oh, I cried there in front of Jordan, and he saw my hurt and cried too because he didn't know or wasn't able to understand till now how I had been feeling. This coming out of me shocked us both, as we knew deep down inside it was—and is—from God.

We also finally came to the conclusion that having children now is not in God's timing. I see now that if God had given me a baby in this caged situation, that baby would definitely make me feel more caged, unable to pursue my destiny, my true calling. I think I got caught up in wanting a baby because I have been so depressed about my current situation. However, as God is revealing to me why I have been burdened and depressed, my desire to walk in his plans is also truly surfacing. It doesn't mean that later he can't bless us in this area, just not now. All that I have been asking God for the past two and a half years has been answered in one conversation. That is incredible! Before I wasn't ready to hear his answers, but now I am. I pray that our next steps will continue to be clear and that Jordan will have the same convictions. Change us, Lord, and continue to change us. I will soon no longer be caged! Amen!

Chapter 4

University Years

I pursued a degree in theology, the study of God, during my days at a small Christian university with hopes of serving as a missionary overseas. My hunger for the Lord was growing as I walked with him daily. I began to ask God questions about the events I read in the book of Acts and how he had worked during that time period. I was drawn to Peter and the other apostles ministering to the lost through healings, signs, and wonders. I read these passages in Scripture in my high school days, but I became hungry to see God work in these ways in my own life. My problem quickly became not being able to easily find the answers that I needed to see these amazing things happen. I was disappointed as my professors in school would not even go near these specific Scriptures with a ten-foot pole to bring understanding to them. But what they did give me were tools and knowledge to begin a search on my own.

My Greek professor had a passion for understanding the Scriptures by studying their root language. His passion (along with the encouragement of other professors for me to pursue digesting all parts of God's Word) allowed a biblical foundation to form in me. I will never forget asking my church history professor after we had studied several theologians what constituted a real theologian. His answer to my surprising question was that theologians studied the Word of God. I then confidently exclaimed that I, too, was a theologian, and he simply smiled. Becoming a theologian, however, was not God's plan for me. In fact, later on in my life, I would learn that theology was one of my enemies and that it would hold me back from fully embracing God and his true character. I am not saying theology in and of itself is bad, but in my life it became a hindrance, a type of religious idol.

In my third year of school, I was introduced to a charismatic group of students that met near my campus for worship. I was, of course, curious to attend and hoped my quickly forming questions about miracles and healings could be answered. I sat through my first ever prayer of deliverance sessions, something I had just discovered people prayed for, and I wept as the couple who led the prayer ministered to me in a way I had never experienced before. They pinpointed things in my life that only God could have led them to point out. In that same prayer session, they prayed for me to be baptized in the Spirit and then waited. Nothing happened. Then they asked me if I could speak in tongues. I looked at them while they were discerning what the Spirit was doing in that room and in me. They further explained that if I could speak in tongues, it would be the Spirit from within speaking through me. Next, they asked me to try to speak to see if I had the gift. I looked at them and instantly knew what they meant. I had felt this leading before as a child when I was crying and shaking after hearing an evangelist speak. But this time I was aware of what the Spirit was trying to do. He was leading me to open my mouth to speak in tongues, but fear and embarrassment kept my mouth shut. I looked at this couple and told them about my experience as a child in that evangelism meeting. But then I told them I had to go home and do this on my own. They respected my decision, and so I ran to my apartment, locked myself in the bathroom, and began to use a gift that had been dormant within me for years. I was able to speak in tongues! *What do I do with this, and who do I share this with?* I thought.

Through conversations I had had in the past and overhearing other students, I knew that this gift was not understood in my circle of friends and acquaintances. Releasing this gift within me excited me, however. I was beginning to live out the book of Acts in my life, and I was thrilled. Everywhere I went, I could not keep from walking in this gift. With my mouth somewhat closed, I had figured out how to silently speak in tongues. I headed back to that same Bible study, ready to learn more a week later. They taught how God still heals today, and I was hungry for what they were sharing. I began to open up to others with what I was learning and was confronted with doubt, concern, and even fear because of this particular charismatic group. Some of the things they were teaching offended people, so I decided to leave that study. But God still used the study to open my eyes up to what he is doing today, and for that I will always be grateful. My reading of Scripture through this new perspective, which subscribed that healings, tongues, and miracles were also for today, changed my walk with God. I asked God how I would grow in these areas. The availability of teachers that were already walking with these gifts and doing so while grounded in the Bible were hard for me to find. I began to feel alone in my journey, and I did not prepare myself at all for what was to come next in my life.

Journal Entry

East Asia
February 7, 2014

Dear Holy Spirit,

I'm writing you to say how terribly sorry I am for having quenched you and for not always listening to you and your direction. I allowed my fear of men and my selfish pursuits to override your voice. You have given me specific gifts that some have refused to acknowledge come from you, and so I have hidden them from others under a false humility. I am sorry for being ashamed and embarrassed of who you have made me to be. I desire to continue to use and grow in these precious gifts as I seek to know Christ. I desire to stand for truth—that these gifts are indeed real and from you. Why you have chosen me to have some of these gifts I will never truly understand, except that you are gracious and merciful. Holy Spirit, help me to honor you before others. Help me live in my gifts freely. I don't want to live a lie anymore. Direct Jordan and me to live in truth and honesty. I am listening, and I am yielding. Again, Holy Spirit, forgive me for hurting you so much and help me forgive others I know will reject me because of your work in me. Make me not afraid of rejection. Strengthen me, Holy Spirit, and please don't pass me up. But instead empower me to be an obedient servant of you. For too long have I lived on the fence, and now I choose to fully immerse myself in all that you have for me. Take me deeper if you will have me. I love you, dear Holy Spirit.

Chapter 5

Seduced into a Never Ending Valley

I am confident that every true child of God will experience seasons of being in a valley. This is a great opportunity for us to lean into God and allow him to mold us and change us. My valley began with an aggressive attack of the enemy that positioned me in a place of vulnerability and made me susceptible to even more attacks. After I went off to school, my relationship with my mother changed. One day we were best friends, and then the next day we became extremely distant. During my first visit home, I was met with anger and distance. The distance I felt with my mother was new for me. I did not know how to respond and left confused as I would go back to school. Soon I saw a pattern. Each time I would return home, I was met with joy and excitement in the beginning, but as my time would draw to an end, my mother would often pick a fight with me. And so I left home often feeling at a loss about what to do. I did not know at the time, but my mother's way of dealing with my growing into a young and independent woman was to push me away. Her silent pain was becoming my new struggle. Anger toward me became her way of guarding her heart from feeling sad when I would leave. This pattern in our relationship would drive a wedge of mistrust between us and hurt my heart.

Along with that struggle, my stepfather's inability to provide for my education financially made him to question if I should continue. My pursuit of a bachelor's degree and ultimately walking out my calling was becoming a battle between me and my parents. In my third year of university, the tension between my parents and me developed into our first episode of estrangement. The constant conflict to finish school was becoming overwhelming for me, and so as they tightened their control over me, I developed the means to survive without their provision.

Once I became financially independent, I took my first opportunity to assert my independence and finally fought back against their control. My parents did not like being challenged, and so I left home broken and wounded. I would not hear from them for a few months. As I would later learn through further conflicts with my parents, setting these healthy boundaries was my way of protecting myself and my fight to become all that God had planned for me. At the time, however, it was a hard blow to the reality of the life God had given me so that he could make me into his likeness. My heart was broken when I realized that those I had trusted and loved the most in my life could hurt me so deeply. And worse yet, these behaviors of hurt were just the beginning of a path filled with them. I was indeed on my own in this life, and I knew I had to be so in order to protect my heart and future. It was all painfully real. I sought help the best I could, but I was too ashamed to let others know about my reality. I was alone, broken, and becoming vulnerable for more attacks.

Of course, I should have run to God, but instead I ran into the arms of another. I allowed myself to look for love in other places, seeking out a relationship with a young man.

My pursuit of a boyfriend left my heart divided. This set me up for even more heartache. After a year of dating a nice Christian boy, he ended our relationship. I put so much energy and care into that relationship that I was blind to his fear of commitment. I allowed him to become an idol for me, and in his mercy and love for me, God took that relationship away. My heart mourned for the loss of that one stable thing in my life. I had never experienced pain on that level before. I had no one to turn to except for my best friend and God. Sadly, God still was not enough for my heart to be satisfied.

By this time in my life, I had graduated from my university and had made two separate trips overseas for missions. God continued to remind me—even in my sufferings—of the promise I had made to him that I would one day serve him as a missionary. I moved back home months after the breakup to start life anew as a college graduate. My heart, still hurting and vulnerable, led me to return home only to continue to struggle with my parents. And instead of fully trusting God, I continued seeking comfort through relationships with boys. For a full year, I purposely walked away from my Creator, feeling angry and hurt that he allowed so much pain and suffering in my life. My struggle to keep out of the reach of my parents' control and feeling desperate to find happiness brought me to a life of merely surviving. My heart was growing hard as a result of my suffering and my lack of forgiveness. I was also seeking self-worth, and the only way I knew how to find it was through my achievements. So an ambition for my boss to recognize me had turned me into a workaholic and I had falsely identified my self-worth by what I did in life. I was changing, but for the worse.

At the end of that year of rebellion against God, I was awakened to a loud knock on my front door early in the morning. It was one of my younger sisters and she was crying. She shared with me about some real struggles she was having in her life and asked me to pray for her. I let her sleep on my couch, and I also went back to bed. I awoke later and saw she had returned back to her home, but then I had another visitor. I was in my bedroom, and I felt deeply sad for my sister. I wanted to cry out to God on her behalf, but I could not. Nevertheless, I got on my knees and face. Then God showed up.

For a full year, I had not prayed to God, worshipped him, or even felt his pulling on my heart. My pain in trials and my sin had clogged all communication pipes with him until that morning. I cried and cried, begging him to forgive me for leaving him. I asked him to forgive the anger I had toward him, and I cried some more. I will never forget the words he spoke into my heart. They were warning words. God warned me to never walk away from him intentionally again, and I trembled in fear as I understood his rebuke to mean I would miss out on a life that he had planned for me. Being at the bottom of my valley, truly broken and repentant, taught me what it meant to be undone in God's presence. None of my pain or anyone else's sins against me ever justifies a life of sin and rebellion. My response to pain was to become numb in my heart, and that meant I was cold toward God. But that visit from God became a renewed hope for me. I had allowed God back into my heart, though he never left me. He was waiting for my return just like the prodigal son parable found in his Word. He waited until I literally was tired of laying in my own filth, until any credit of my own righteousness in my life was gone, and until I saw no hope in a life without him. He waited for me to look up at him. Our God is a jealous God.

Tabitha Crusoe

Journal Entry

East Asia
February 12, 2014

I see myself speaking with Jesus, telling him how I don't understand my calling fully. I ask him who my audience is and who I will be ministering to. What will I be doing, and how will I fully walk in it? He just smiles at me in response. Then he takes oil and pours it over my head, anointing me with purity. I feel it being poured and dripping down my head and onto my shoulders. I ask him, "Why purity?" He says, "Because the pure in heart shall see God." I tell him, "I want to see you with my eyes one day." He says I will. Although my head is swirling with questions about understanding my calling, Jesus, however, is not too concerned with my questions. He does listen to them with love. His anointing me with purity is so big because of my past sins. I receive the anointing! He is showing me that even though I don't have all the answers now, it doesn't mean he isn't still working in me.

Chapter 6

Carried by God Out of a Valley

was lured away from God by the enemy through an open door of pain in my heart, and the strength to seek healing and be set free from the enemy's strongholds was going to have to come from God. God was strict with me as a parent would be after a child had returned home from running off with a bunch of hooligans. In all of his strictness, however, I felt his intense love for me and desire to see me whole in him. I began to remove myself from the influences in my life that had sought to corrupt me. I distanced myself from friends that brought with them lifestyles I could no longer live. I quit a job that kept seducing my heart to live for the purpose of attaining success, money, and titles. I had to cut out the movies, music, and all media that would easily have entangled me with the world. Through the leading of the Holy Spirit, I began to reconcile with my parents and the old friends I had dropped when I walked away from God. The new job I found was simple and did not use too much of my energy, but it gave me what I needed during this season of pruning. It gave me time, and joyfully, I used that time to think, pray, and digest any spiritual nourishment I could get my hands on or afford. My new job also took away a hunger for identity found in what I did rather than being a child of God. This season was not easy for me, but I love to look back and smile, remembering a time when I loved God with a love I had no idea could come out of my heart. I understood the woman washing Jesus's feet with her hair and weeping tears. I understood how to be forgiven for so much, results in loving God and accepting his mercy deeply. I realized then that although I had sinned greatly and had broken God's heart in my turning away from him, in his love for me, God brought me to know him in a new way. He showed me how his character also included being a patient, forgiving, and kind deity. He showed me more of his nature, and within his holy presence, I saw more of my need for him.

As if that season of brokenness was not enough, God had in mind to position me where pruning and growth would be difficult to escape. One afternoon at my parents' home, I fell asleep on the couch while my mother was washing dishes. During my nap, the Lord spoke to me with a clear and vivid dream. He showed me an airplane and people boarding it, including myself. I heard his Spirit speak into mine. He instructed me to follow through with my high school commitment of serving him overseas. I awoke with those words ringing in my heart, and after sharing my dream with my mother, I made an appointment to see our church's missions pastor.

I soon reconnected with a missionary I had met during college on a short-term trip. She was seeking out people who were interested in coming to East Asia to work alongside of her, teach English at a university, and of course, engage with the students with God's gospel. She received my resume, which I quickly put together. I had no teaching experience, but by God's grace, I was hired by an East Asian university to teach spoken English. And as exciting as that open door was for me, it brought me much grief and anxiety because I was to begin my new job that following fall semester. At the time I decided to go, it was already the month of May. I had only three and a half months to get my life in order, which included moving out of my apartment, moving into my parents' home, selling my television, giving away my cat, and giving my car payments and car over to my parents. I also had to prepare my heart for a yearlong absence from my family.

The whirlwind of that summer never ceases to amaze me as people were raised up by God to help prepare me. My home church committed to providing me with some greatly needed financial support, and a small group adopted me as the missionary they wanted to support through prayer and whatever else I needed. My younger sister had a two-year-old boy I dearly loved, and only one year prior, my mother had had a baby I also hated to leave behind. I spent lots of time crying before God as each step I needed to take in order to go overseas to East Asia took from me great energy and required real courage and faith. I had none of those things, so my cries to God only increased the closer I got to the date of my departure. I was so vulnerable and needy, and I knew that I was not ready for this change, but I could not ignore God's clear direction for my life. It would not be until years later that I would learn how God's purpose for his children is to make them aware of their need for him in order for them to walk in perfect step with him.

Journal Entry

East Asia
February 13, 2014

The Lord wants to work on my identity, an identity according to his Word and not man's. He is telling me to see myself as he does through his eyes. I see Jesus sitting with me, looking into the sun. He enjoys its warmth and light. He looks at me and calls me a prophet just like David. Not a teacher or trainer but a prophet. He tells me to build my identity from there. *Begin with prophet and build on it.* He says that I can't walk in my gifting fully until I embrace this as my identity. If I doubt this is for me, then the gifting is stifled and cannot grow. He assures me that this is who he made me to be. He wants me to study what a prophet is, not just a seer. I struggle with embracing what I know is deep inside of me. Jesus is being very clear, and I choose to believe him. However, I feel terribly humbled and hope in time that my confidence in my prophetic gift will grow. David was a king, but first, he was a prophet because of his intimate relationship with God. The Holy Spirit spoke through David, and Peter called David a prophet. Lord, help me understand more on this and confirm it through your Word. Would you really choose me to have a prophetic gift? Why? Why me? I need my thinking changed. Renew my mind, Jesus.

Chapter 7

God Opens My Eyes

I t was a gorgeous and bright Sunday morning years ago when my best friend and I were listening to our Bible teacher. Sadly, I cannot remember what she was specifically teaching on, but I do remember she lightly touched on the subject of seeing angels and visions with our physical eyes. That sparked an interesting conversation I had with my friend afterward. I vividly remember during our conversation exclaiming how I never wanted to see an angel because it would horrify me if I did. I do not know if you believe God has a sense of humor or not, but in that same week, I sure did find he indeed has one. It was still around one month before I would journey to East Asia, and so by this time I had already moved in with my parents and my new baby sister. I was living in my old high school bedroom, but with a lot more belongings that I had slowly collected over the years.

One night I was awakened by the Holy Spirit from a dream. The dream itself truly amazed me as I found myself in flight within the eye of a huge tornado, and I was held up by my arms on both sides by two angels. These were not small cupid angels mind you, but beautiful and strong angels. As the Holy Spirit woke me up from this dream, I felt either my body or my spirit being laid down on my bed, and almost simultaneously, as I opened my physical eyes, I saw a hand lifting up from them. This hand had removed something that had covered my spiritual eyes, and I was allowed to see a vision of angel wings right above my head. The wings were too many to count, and they shimmered brightly in my dark room. Of course, I was frightened and unsure of what was going on, so I turned on my lamp and sat up in bed. The vision by this time had disappeared, and I sat there with tears in my eyes. God had opened my eyes to see the army of angels that fought in his name to protect me. Surely, I was not venturing to East Asia on my own.

I did not know what to do with this experience. *Should I tell others? Should I keep it a secret? Does this change how I talk with God?* I felt completely humbled that God would show me this, and I could not understand why he did this. But I took it as what it was, a comfort and encouragement for me as I was preparing for East Asia. I did choose to tell my mother, and after seeing her speechless response, I decided to keep this one between me and God unless he directed me otherwise.

Later I would be able to understand how the hand lifting off of my eyes was simply the Holy Spirit removing a blinding spirit so that my spiritual eyes would be able to see into the spirit realm. I would also learn quickly that this was not a one-time experience for me, but it was the beginning of walking in the spiritual gift of discernment. As I have been taught by the Holy Spirit on this specific gifting, my ability to discern and see into the spirit realm has grown. However, it has taken me years to learn to walk in this gifting because I never sat under another teacher to learn from them. I did not share with many about these things and oftentimes asked God to provide me with someone who could understand

and help me. I was compelled for many years to search out others who had this same gifting so that I could grow and learn, but to no avail.

The greatest result of this experience and gifting of discernment had only created more of a thirst and hunger in me to know God and be in his presence always. I have never sought after visions, tongues, or dreams, but only after God, who blesses his children with them to advance his kingdom and name. In fact, I went through a season while in East Asia, where God stopped my ability to see in the spirit realm and to have dreams. I then leaned into his Word more to hear from him and continued to grow in my relationship with him. God was testing my heart, and I am thankful he does. I do not ever want to desire a gifting more than I desire God. I want to be so close to God that if I were unable to have dreams and visions, I still would not miss a step with him. I want to always be madly in love with my God.

Journal Entry

East Asia
February 16, 2014

I see myself ice-skating on a huge lake, solid and crisp ice beneath me. My skating is beautiful and strong and fast. It represents what's within me that desperately wants out. I'm twirling and skating swiftly, and no one is around to tell me to stop or criticize me or dash my dreams. I have on a gorgeous dress that flows long and wide in the wind. A separate wind—other than the wind I create by my own skating—blows all around me and gives me greater delight and strength as I continue to perform. I feel free and joyful because what has been trapped inside of me is finally being released. My heart yearns and aches as I see this vision. I yearn to have this freedom because what is inside of me is growing restless. A stirring of the Holy Spirit is becoming stronger each day, a stirring to release what God has put in me. I ache because now I am aware of how I had been bound by the enemy. I know the Lord has cut the ropes, but I'm still waiting, waiting for my day of release and pure freedom in him. As I wait, I am anguished and at times impatient for that day to arrive. I yearn for it so much and feel so cramped in the box I have allowed myself to live in. I want out. I want to scream. I want to run and burst open the doors to God's destiny for my life! But still, I have to wait, yet I'm burning inside. Will this burning burn me up? Or will God grant me freedom from my agony, my pain, my hurt, and my shame? Still, I wait.

Chapter 8

Boot Camp

B efore I go any further, I need to explain how during my first trip to East Asia, a short mission trip that only took two weeks, I realized how much I disliked what I experienced of the culture, the language, the food, and the constant stares from curious locals, basically everyone. However, I met two East Asian university students I really liked, and I was able to share Christ with them. So when I set foot on East Asian territory to be a light for Christ for an entire year that fall, I came face-to-face with culture shock, one of the new enemies I would face while in East Asia.

The Lord used my time in East Asia to mature me, grow me in him, mold and shape me, create a deeper love in me for evangelism and obedience, and teach me how to fight new enemies. Most of those enemies were personal for me, such as dealing with loneliness, fear, selfishness, discontentment, homesickness, and doubt. Enemies like these God wanted uprooted out of my heart. He had brought me to East Asia to learn and grow in his special spiritual boot camp. I call it boot camp because when I thought I had finally conquered an enemy, a new one would rise, and I felt like the spiritual training would never end.

At the same time that God was allowing enemies to surface in my life against the backdrop of living and working in the spiritually dry land of East Asia, he was also graciously allowing me to impact the lives of many students. The sweet nature of an East Asian student is contagious. That is why anyone who goes to East Asia to do student ministry usually falls in love with it. What was even more contagious was watching that student fall in love with Jesus. Their purpose in life grew from just trying to get an education in hopes of finding marriage and a job to loving their Creator and serving him. God was using East Asia to break my heart. I did not struggle as hard with culture shock anymore, and at the end of my first year in East Asia, I decided to extend my stay.

Journal Entry

East Asia
February 22, 2014

Dear Lord,

I desperately want and hunger for the freedom I felt in the dream you blessed me with. That taste of freedom will never leave my spirit, my soul. You imprinted it in my inner being in order for me to cry out to you more. Let your will be done! Grant Jordan and me that freedom that brings joy—great joy in the freedom to obey you entirely. If that freedom is not given to us, I will surely go to my grave never having the opportunity to serve you in my fullest ability and capacity! Please, please, I beg you, O God, do not overlook us, and let your pleasing will be done in our lives. I am so sorry for never having listened to your direction in the first place when we sought how to come overseas. But I know you allowed this, and you will use our wrong choices for your glory and for our understanding of freedom and the true hunger to know and walk with you more. Don't ever leave me, Holy Spirit. Don't look away from me, Lord Jesus. Here am I. Send me!

Chapter 9

Faced with a Real Enemy

The last six months of my spiritual boot camp experience in East Asia brought me face-to-face with a physical enemy, the law of East Asia. Working for universities in East Asia, you are given a university officer who is responsible for your well-being and who also makes certain that you fulfill your duties as laid out in the contract you signed when taking the job. Simply put, they are responsible that you keep to the law written for foreigners residing in their country. From day one I had a special relationship with my officer. She looked for any opportunity to get me in trouble with my boss at the university. Therefore, I sought out opportunities to show her love and kindness. She knew I was a Christian early on because another foreign teacher had asked if I was one within earshot of her, and since that day, she became relentless in revealing my true intentions as a teacher on their campus. It definitely felt like a game of cat and mouse while I served there, but God kept me covered by his hand.

My officer's pursuit of me became more and more ridiculous. Living on campus brought many unannounced visits and strange questions from her. One time a teammate of mine found her walking up our building stairwell. My teammate lived right across from me and knew right away our officer's intentions with being in our building. She also knew I was in the middle of a Bible study in my apartment, where several students sat listening to me teach. So my teammate quickly sent me a text message and then proceeded to distract our university officer by inviting her into her apartment so that I could quietly dismiss my students without anyone noticing. Having teammates who served God together with me on that campus was a huge blessing, as we all looked out for one another as best we could.

I could share more stories similar to that one, but I would rather move on and talk about a time of persecution that changed my understanding of many things. During the summer before my last semester in East Asia, my officer saw me on campus and walked up to me. She was uncharacteristically nice to me, which surprised me. As we were talking, she mentioned casually how she was about to go on a trip to go and meet some new foreign teachers that were coming in the fall. She also mentioned how a colleague of hers had backed out on the trip and asked me if I would like to accompany her to pick up the new foreign teachers. Since our relationship was not always smooth, I thought this trip with her might improve it. I also knew of a couple of friends who were traveling through that same city on the exact same days she was planning on being there. I asked my team leader if I should go on this trip, and she encouraged me to do so. However, while away with my officer on a train to another city, another colleague of hers searched my apartment. My officer had given her a key to my apartment.

I realized something was wrong when my officer started acting very ugly to me on our return to our university. She had just found out that I had in my possession two suitcases full of Bibles in the local language. They took pictures and showed them to the local community communist party group. My officer was so furious with me that upon returning to our city after riding an overnight train, she eagerly looked for an opportunity to get me alone and corner me. After a quick bite together near campus, the new foreign teachers stepped out to buy some cigarettes, and she turned toward me and began yelling at me. She quickly questioned me about who I was with and what was I doing there. I sensed on the train something was wrong with the change in her attitude toward me, but I never imagined a bold confrontation as this.

By God's grace alone, I remained calm and answered all her questions the best way I knew how. I told her I was not affiliated with any missionary agency, which was true, and I was there to teach English, another truth. I also had quietly texted my teammates our planned emergency text when we were in trouble as I held my phone under the table. My officer's face grew red as she angrily listened to my short answers. Thankfully, the other foreign teachers returned and her attention was diverted to them with a fake smile. We all walked together toward campus, and she led us to the foreign teacher apartment buildings. Once again, she decided to confront me with more accusations when the other teachers had gone inside their new homes. She then marched me to my apartment front door where a dear local brother was waiting for my return. Seeing that her opportunity to badger me even more had been denied, my officer abruptly stormed off. I was relieved as God's intervention came through a visiting friend, who really just wanted to see the scores of the NBA finals on my television.

My team leaders gathered myself and our team in one location that evening to discuss the events that were taking place. They were the ones who received the information about why I was harshly confronted. And they gave us instruction on how to quickly remove all of the Bibles in my apartment before a real search by the authorities would take place.

What was really interesting to me, however, was that only a week and a half prior to this search of my apartment, I was saying good-bye to a team of high school students from the States who had brought all of these Bibles. At that time I had only one night to receive these Bibles and find a good hiding place for them. Most of my team was gone on individual trips, so I had no choice but to hide them in my apartment until my teammates came back to help with distributing them. Yet within that short time period, my apartment was searched. I was careful in how I had them brought to my apartment so that it did not look suspicious, but still, someone was watching closely and waiting for an opportunity to catch me.

Journal Entry

East Asia
March 10, 2014

Today, while at our hotel on vacation, Jordan and I were given a key to an iron-barred gate that led us onto the beach. Prior to getting the right key for the lock, we were first given the wrong key and could not open the gate. As I waited for Jordan to get the right key, I heard the Spirit telling me that he had given us the keys to our freedom. I looked through the barred and locked gate and saw the beautiful beach with white sand and clear water on the other side. I longed to be out on the beach, and I could not hold in my excitement when Jordan finally opened the gate.

The keys are released in the spirit realm and have yet to be given in the physical, yet it is only a matter of time when they will be given. Jordan will receive the keys, and he will need to make the choices to open the gate to our freedom. He is the head of our family, and so it makes sense that today he was the one getting the key for the gate. I tried to unlock the gate myself, and I could not. This is prophetic in how God will use Jordan to lead our family in deliverance out of our current situation.

Throughout this day God showed me his beautiful creation underwater, his promised symbol the rainbow, and he gave me a visual of being free in him through observing kiteboarders. Each enjoyment had its own level of risk, challenges, and lessons needed in order to fully enjoy the activity. I want to learn kiteboarding and told him I did. He told me in response that the level of risk and strength it would take is symbolic of the level of risk and strength it will take to enjoy him in relationship more deeply. He told me that he is willing to teach me if I am willing to take the risk and challenge. I am willing! The freedom it felt to go snorkeling today was fantastic, but I have an itch for even greater freedom to kite across the waves, completely directed wherever the wind moves. Of course, the kiteboarder has some control, but only the ability to move the kite so that it will pick up the movement of the wind. I see that as an exact picture of walking deeper in relationship with God. I still have freedom to choose God's direction, but I have no control over the wind and its strength and movement, the Holy Spirit. Before the kiteboarder begins, he sets his kite ready flying in the wind and prepares himself to be lifted up on his board. Sometimes he allows the wind to pick him up off the water. It is truly amazing to watch the huge kite in all its bright and vivid colors flying in the air. Nothing is more beautiful until you see a coast full of kiteboarders freely enjoying their rides.

Chapter 10

Head Games

Your adrenaline sure does race for days as you walk through unknown and dangerous territory. It was obvious that I had been marked as a threat on my campus. Although all the Bibles were relocated safely, I was still waiting for my university to call me in and question me. My team leaders, dear servants of the Lord, advised me to keep my distance with those who could be treated worse than I would be if they were caught along with me. This meant keeping away from teammates who would be treated harshly if connected with me too closely, and our team did consist of other non-American foreigners who did not have US passports to bail them out of serious trouble. It also meant that I had to keep away from the local brothers and sisters I had the privilege of leading to the Lord, my spiritual children. So I isolated myself, and even though I tried to make new friends with students on campus, the school had isolated me by warning the students about me.

My emotions ranged from fear to loneliness, grief, and rejection every single day in those last months. Soon the university began to respond to the summer's raid of my apartment and brought in the local police to instruct and warn all of the foreign teachers of the law in East Asia about us. It did not take the other foreign teachers long to realize why we were being treated this way, and soon they turned on my teammates and me in their own way. Sadly, two of these foreign teachers were also Christians who criticized me and another teammate for our boldness with the gospel.

This brought doubt and confusion to my heart. By breaking the law in East Asia, had I jeopardized other lives? Did God disapprove of my ignoring the authorities in East Asia? I fearfully grappled with these questions and the fact that I had been warned by another missionary that I might be questioned by the authorities. She shared with me that the worst thing that could take place is that they would bang on my apartment door at midnight to scare me and bring me in for questioning. The thought of this made me tremble, and I feared going to sleep at night after that. I continued to teach my classes, but I waited for the university and or the local government to make their move against me.

After a month of waiting (without being able to do any ministry work), I still had not been personally confronted. During this month, however, I drew close with the Lord. He had answered all of my questions, showing me his Word from Peter and John's statements regarding obeying God rather than men, and teaching me much about conquering this very tangible fear I had through worshipping him. These lessons and many more did not become instilled in me overnight, but walking into fire and meeting the Lord there cannot be experienced without real change in your inner being. I had never felt such sweet fellowship with the Lord as I did during this season, and the growth of learning his character and faithfulness amazed me. Trials and persecutions give us the opportunity to know God more, and the heat of the situation causes the surfacing of impurities and flaws the Lord wants to remove from us. I am not saying I walked out of that fire perfect. I am just saying that I did come out a little stronger and more aware of my need to love God.

Journal Entry

East Asia
March 13, 2014

I see Jesus sitting across from me and telling me again that trouble will come into our lives soon, but he also tells me to trust him and hold onto him. He understands every emotion we will experience because he went through trouble too. He looks out at the kiteboarders with me. The more I watch them, the more I want to learn, but I am not prepared to learn on this trip. Jesus says this parallels my own life. He has already given me the key to my freedom, and here in this place I go through the gate and observe the kiteboarders; however, I still return back behind the gate, apprehensive and not ready to learn.

This is where I am in my freedom process. I have the key, and I have ventured out in freedom. But I am not prepared yet to walk out in freedom and live freely and not return to my life behind the comfortable locked gate. Watching the kiteboarding entices me. I want to be a part of what they are doing, but it comes at a great cost. My desire to do ministry apart from our organization comes first from watching others serve in their freedom. They, too, entice me. The Lord has given me a physical visual so that I can see what he is doing and has been doing in my heart and life. He has been preparing me. Moving me and Jordan from the comfort of being behind the locked gate as observers will take something radical. In fact, it will take a storm to get us in the right place.

God is so faithful to prepare my heart for things to come, and I am humbled by his love for me. Jesus, I am not afraid of the trouble that will come because I know you have ordained it. I know I need it to prepare me more for my freedom to come. I also know that the next time I get to come here, I will be prepared physically and spiritually to walk in all you have for me. I will learn kiteboarding! Amen!

Chapter 11

The Last Card Played

My university officer was desperate now to have me removed from my teaching position, and so she arranged for a student of mine to write a false letter against me and send it to the vice president of the university. I assumed that the photographs of the Bibles in my apartment had been taken illegally, and so the photos could not be used as evidence against me. And with the removal of all materials that could get me in trouble, no one could find any new evidence. My waiting finally ended when another foreign teacher and I were called into our boss's office. I showed up after the other teacher and walked into the office, calm and held together by God.

My boss was a gentle man in his early thirties, and he never had intimidated me before. He sat at his desk across from two chairs, and the other teacher sat in one of them. I took the empty seat beside her. Soon our university officer joined us and stood against the office wall with a strange and almost evil smile on her face. Our boss began to ask a question, and before he finished his sentence, the foreign teacher beside me began to cry and exclaim that she had done nothing wrong. Our boss told her she could leave.

Then I realized that she had only been called in along with me to make my confrontation somewhat easier on me. I actually was relieved they let her go. I felt horrible that they had scared her for my ease and comfort. After she left the office, my boss then asked my officer to leave as well. Of course, she was not happy to leave, but this reminded and comforted me that her authority only went so far. My boss had greater authority than her, and I was sure glad about that. The conversation between us was calm but not pleasant. I was nervous until I saw small flashes of white lights dancing behind my boss. I felt peace from the Holy Spirit and knew without a doubt that he was enabling me to see that my boss and I were not the only ones in that office. We were accompanied by angels.

My boss shared the details about the letter sent to the vice president, and he calmly asked me if I had taught about Jesus in the classroom. I had not done so, and I answered no. I was then asked if I had taught Jesus to students in my apartment, and I answered yes. Then I further explained that I was a Christian and that I desired to share my life with my students, and of course, that included my faith. My boss responded by ignoring my answer and explanation as if he had not heard my confession at all. He then proceeded to remind me not to teach about Jesus to my students. Still, to this day, I wonder if God covered my boss's ears during that questioning time because he simply never showed any response to me and my words. Instead he encouraged me and talked about my skills as a teacher, showing me that favor rested on my shoulders while seated before my enemies that day. I walked away from that meeting with my job still intact and with a bounce in my step. God was not done with my service there yet.

A few weeks went by, and I sensed the Lord leading me to break my teaching contract since I was unable to make any move forward in ministry there. It was still dangerous to meet with my local brothers and sisters, and some were being pressured by their university teachers to stop meeting as a church. My officer kept watching me closer, showing up now in my English classes and at other times to my apartment. I made a decision to leave the school by the end of that semester and return home to the States for a much-needed rest. I was emotionally and spiritually exhausted, and I felt more alone because I was no longer able to see my local brothers and sisters.

About a month before the end of that fall semester, I went back to my boss and played my last card. There had always been the fear that the university could still fire me right at the end so that I could not get another teaching job within the city. It was difficult for me, not knowing if or when they would play this calculated move. It also gave them room to still bring the authorities in, and I did not want this to go to that level at all. I sat before my boss and told him I was leaving, and he easily let me go. He knew his own job was now on the line because of me and had expressed that to me in our last meeting. I told him I did not want to have anyone lose their job on account of me. He understood what I meant. The school waived my penalty fee for breaking my contract, and my boss shed a few tears with the reality of losing me. He said that I was one of their best English teachers and that all the students loved my classes. Then he invited me back in the future to look him and his family up and pay them a visit. He said I was always welcome.

Journal Entry

East Asia
March 18, 2014

Jesus reminds me of a vision he had given me before. I was riding a horse through beautiful fields, and he was riding the horse through me. He is now saying that every day he wants to live through me in the same way. He wants me to visualize seeing him ministering to others rather than myself. Today during lunch I saw a young local man order his food and then watched him limp slowly to his seat. Right away the Spirit told me he was recently in an electric bike accident, and the Spirit then instructed me to pray for him.

The Spirit was on me strong and clearly told to me to go to the young man. What happened next shocked me. I finished my meal, stood up, gathered my things, and bravely took one step toward this young man. After that, it wasn't me walking toward the young man. It was Jesus. My mind was aware that the Spirit had taken over. I sat down and easily began to talk with this young man, and he was willing to let me pray for him. The first step was uncomfortable and fearful, but after that, I had God's boldness, courage, and power to minister to him. In fact, he had been in an electric bike accident along with his friend. He had injured his leg, but his friend's leg had been injured worse. His parents were believers, and so I shared a little with him about the gospel. I shared only what I heard Jesus tell me, and then I stood up to leave. He stood up to shake my hand in response. I told him that Jesus loved him and that God loves him and wants a relationship with him. He said he loved God too. The first step of faith is us. The next step is Jesus. The first step tells Jesus that you are willing for him to work through you. Help me be more and more willing, Lord.

Chapter 12

Finishing Strong

With only one month left before I would head back to the States, I decided to make the most of my time. I had not been able to speak the gospel to any student for fear I would get into more trouble. Therefore, my hunger to share was even greater. It was still unsafe for my students who had already become Christians, especially if they were connected to me, and so I left them in the care of one of my teammates.

I was told to stop sharing about Jesus with my students or I would lose my job, but now that the fear of getting into trouble for sharing my faith was no longer an issue with me, I put together a plan. I would become the real threat that the university had already assigned me to be. My plan was to share with the 150 students I was teaching. I asked each student to organize in groups of fifteen and to come to my apartment to get to know their teacher better. From all of the gossip on campus about my predicament, they all already knew I was in East Asia as a missionary. They were aware that coming to my apartment would involve listening to me share about my faith. I would then pray over each student's name who signed up the afternoon before they arrived, and

I would ask God for boldness. Every student came willingly to my apartment, curious about the threat I posed to their lives. And all they discovered was the love God had for them through the death and resurrection of his Son.

Another like-minded East Asian teacher in the university needed a substitute for his English class, and during that last month, he came and asked me if I would teach two of his classes. I agreed, and in those classes I also invited all of the students to my apartment as well, and they were eager to come. By the end of the semester, by God's grace and strength, I had shared the gospel with more than two hundred students. Even old students from semesters before would show up to these gatherings because they had heard I was going home soon as a result of my faith. Each time I shared, my courage and boldness to share only increased, and I always gave an invitation for them to receive Jesus into their lives. No one made a decision. I was okay with that because I had been obedient to God, and I knew other workers would water those seeds I had planted as these students lived their lives. My marathon of sharing had changed me and torn down a wall of fear that my students had of me and that I had of authority. The school never responded to my actions of boldness. They overlooked it because they knew I was soon going home. Yet in his love and faithfulness to me, God blessed me beyond measure after months of silence. He gave me strength and power to open my mouth once again.

In the morning of the day I was set to return to the States, I was packed and ready to leave at 5:00 a.m. for the small airport. I had made many friends in this city, and one of them was a young taxi driver I would call if I needed a ride. He was going to be my driver that morning. I looked at my apartment one last time and heard a familiar voice at my door. It was my university officer coming to get my keys and check the apartment. I opened the door, and she came sweeping in. Then several students came up the stairs behind her to come and say good-bye to me. I was surprised with how early they got up to come and see me off. They helped me with my luggage downstairs, and as I was walking out the building toward my young driver friend, I was welcomed by many more students!

My brothers and sisters I had not been able to minister to throughout the past semester were all there. Students from my English classes were also there, and all came to say farewell. One of the local brothers came up to me, crying in the midst of all the good-byes. He said he now knew Jesus because of me. I quickly turned red and anxiously rounded my head to see if my officer was within earshot. She was there, standing right behind me, frustrated with all the students who had come to see me off. I looked back at the student and decided to let him keep talking because I knew my officer needed to hear his heart too. I got in the car, and two dear local brothers rode along with me to the airport. Because I had yet to learn to speak their language, they came to translate for me, and they wanted to see me off at the airport. My driver asked me if he could drive me back to America, but I had to explain to him that it was too far for him to drive. The sincerity of his question made me smile.

My heart broke as I boarded my plane. I had no idea how I had impacted their lives till that early morning, and I was terribly sad to leave them all. However, the greatest impact was definitely made in my own heart. I had little doubt that I would return again one day. In fact, I gave God my word that if he desired it, I would return to serve East Asia again. God used the students of East Asia to open my eyes to the little opportunity they had in hearing the gospel. In his mercy God let me see the East Asians through his eyes, something I had not expected to happen.

Tabitha Crusoe

Journal Entry

East Asia
March 31, 2014

I had a dream the other night that my dog and I were running late for a scheduled plane ride. We made it through check-in and security only to show up at our gate one second late. The gate closed as we were running up to it and the flight attendant said she could not reopen it. It was closed. I fell to my knees, crying in anguish for them to please open the gate. I awoke from that dream, still feeling the anguish and desperation.

That day and the day prior, I had been crying out to God in brokenness about our situation. Although our meeting time with another missionary couple was extremely encouraging, it had triggered something deep inside me that surfaced all of this pain. After sharing openly about the spiritual giftings I walked in, my dear friends continued to accept and love me. In contrast, however, it showed how much Jordan had not accepted me in the same way. After my dream I heard the Spirit tell me two words—plane and passenger. I looked those up in my dream dictionary and learned that a plane symbolizes international ministry and a passenger symbolizes how your life is at the mercy of another's decisions and leading. God was telling me that I was going to miss out on what he has for us because I was a passenger and my pilot was not making the right decisions. This scared me a great deal and compelled me to talk with Jordan. After a hard talk and tears on both sides, God showed Jordan his error in not fully accepting me as the Lord had made me. Yesterday we were brought to a fork in the road of our lives, and God showed me his faithfulness in speaking clearly to Jordan.

Chapter 13

And Two Become One

While I was in East Asia, I met the man I would later marry. He was on a different team in a different city, but he had the same supervisor that I had. The supervisor I am talking about is the same missionary who recruited me to come and serve. At first, interest was one-sided. I took notice of him and all of his handsome features and his laid-back personality. He towered over me in height, and I was mesmerized by his eyes and smile. When he did begin to notice me in return, our short courtship brought us to a shorter engagement and then marriage.

However, prior to our engagement, my faith in God's plan and provision for my life was tested as my future spouse's fear of commitment began to surface. I had already been terribly heartbroken once before in my life by a young man, and I was not going to risk another broken heart. This time around I went to God and asked him to guard my heart and to help me know how to respond to these signs of fear of commitment. The year before God had given me a dream about this man being my husband, and God had tested my faith as I waited for this man to pursue me. But now God was challenging my trust in him once again through another dream that contradicted the first. This second dream showed me releasing my future spouse into a moving river with no confidence that he would return to me. God was telling me to break up with Jordan and to release him, so I did. Thankfully, the breakup did not become our ultimate fate. It took only one night for Jordan to recognize that his fear was coming between himself and God's desire for him to be married. The next day he was ready to move forward in our relationship, and three weeks later he proposed.

I realized that change came to my situation because I chose to trust God's promises. Had I clung onto the relationship as I had done in my past, I would have been robbed of God's best for me. Trusting God meant following his lead instead of my own, and as painful as it was to obey him, it truly saved me from a whole mess of heartache in the end. After we were married, I finally shared these two dreams with my husband. He was grateful for God's faithfulness in our relationship. We would remain in the States for the first three years of our marriage before heading out as a team to serve together in East Asia again.

Journal Entry

East Asia
June 23, 2014

I have been having a lot of dreams about my past, all involving when and how a stronghold had entered my life. Last night I dreamed of my sisters and me when we were younger and sharing a room together. Our house was repeatedly broken into, and a thief stole so much of our valuable belongings. Then I dreamed of the same house, but this time I was married and only living with my husband.

The same thief that came when I was young broke in again and stole from me. Jordan and another unidentified man, however, caught the thief this time! The thief was a small boy, but he was very mean. Jordan and the man made this boy return everything that he had stolen from me. He even found the things he had taken from me during my childhood. It was all returned! God is showing me that he will redeem to me all that was stolen by the enemy throughout my life! Amen!

Chapter 14

Returning to East Asia

Serving on the field as half of a married couple compared to serving as a single young woman brings a whole new bag of surprises and challenges to the work. When you are young and single, you can place all of your energy and time into the lives you are serving. Having a spouse that you must learn to work with pulls away some of your attention on the work and puts it on a relationship that requires time and energy as well. This results in learning to manage time well, communicating clearly, and really being flexible. Our decision as a newly married couple to begin our new lives together in the States instead of quickly moving overseas turned out to be a wise one. Around six months on the field together, we began to realize how never having worked together before and now seeing one another all day long most days was a huge transition for our marriage. Experiences we had not had before because we worked separate jobs and only saw one another at the end of the day were testing our patience and surfacing some character issues we did not know existed in both of us.

My husband's parents were in a time of transition as well. My father-in-law retired from a long forty-year career and was now spending his days at home where my mother-in-law grew anxious because she was unaccustomed to a life with a retired spouse. The transition was more difficult than they had imagined. As my husband and I listened to their transitional woes, it dawned on us that we ourselves were experiencing very similar things, but of course, without the retirement part. We were learning to live together in a life where we needed to become less selfish and more supportive, understanding, and caring for one another. When two lives are both going through transition together along with embracing culture issues on the field, the two individuals can choose to work together or eat each other alive because of their high-stress levels. For my husband and me, both of whom were growing weary of our frequent arguments, we slowly began to yield to God's plan for us as a couple serving together. We soon learned that God's plan was not to just supernaturally fix the things we disliked in our spouse but to use our marriage relationship to prune off of us our own individual ugliness. God used our marriage and still does to better equip us to serve him.

Once we stopped fighting God in this process, our marriage relationship began to grow stronger and deeper. And our relationship with God grew as well. Today we laugh together as we are able to compare our relationship when on the field with retired couples who have had to learn to live together as well. We still have very independent personalities, but we are so used to being around one another that we get separation anxiety when one of us has to leave on a trip for a few days. We have also learned how to recognize in each other when we need to be alone or when we need rest. We do not take offense toward one another as easily as we used to, and although we worked together most days, we still made time to have rest and fun together. What could have become a burden if we had not been open is now our greatest joy. We have the privilege to serve the Lord together.

Journal Entry

East Asia
July 8, 2014

This last week has been challenging in dealing with an early miscarriage as well as realizing that I have had at least five early miscarriages over the past three years. I am thankful to the Lord for learning this, yet I am still processing it all. For Jordan and me, our greatest concern is my health. We calculated last night that I have spent an entire year of my life sick. That's a long time, and because that time of being sick has spanned off and on over the last four years, I have had difficulty moving forward physically, mentally, and emotionally. I have been greatly distracted from living life fully. It has been a difficult time and season for us in our lives. Yet we are thankful and grateful for God's healing power in my life.

We made a decision last night to not pursue having children right now in order for us to move on with life and be of use to the Lord. What does life look like for a married couple that cannot have children? What plans does God have for us since bearing children is not the plan? Is there something I cannot see yet? I believe God has a plan, he has not overlooked us. He knew this would be our situation, and I know he will prove himself faithful still. I mourn not being a mother and Jordan not being a father. I am terribly sad, but I cannot go on in life holding tightly onto something that perhaps God is withholding for purposes unknown. He knows my heart best. I trust the Lord with this part of my life, and I hope for the best yet to come.

Chapter 15

Lessons on the Field

When I began writing this book, my husband and I had already served on the mission field together for five years. Separately, we also had served for a time. He had served three years as a single adult, and I had served a year and a half as a single adult. We imagined many more years on the field together; however, we have learned how God is the authority and planner of our lives, and his plans will ultimately be the ones that trump ours. It comes as no surprise that our time spent serving East Asians has included many great life lessons, more than I can share in just one chapter.

In regards to ministry, we had slowly embraced the messiness of ministering to people. When we worked in secular jobs in the States, our progress and success was measured by productivity, but on the field building relationships, we found that we had difficulty measuring our efforts. We invested time and energy in lives that may or may not have accepted Christ as their Savior, and if they did, we were not always able to make them *strong* disciples of Christ. Our schedules changed weekly as we made appointments, worked on projects meant to sow seeds in people, invested in and discipled brothers and sisters, and prepared for trainings. We hosted teams from the States throughout the year, and these seasons became an investment in hopeful future missionaries who may or may not return to the field and serve like we did. In short, we have learned that as vessels of the Lord, we had no way of controlling our success on the field. The only thing we could bring to the table was faith in God and our work and prayer interceding for so many. The rest was out of our hands.

If we tried to take more control of our work through becoming busier, we always failed as our efforts did not honor the Lord. We were not allowing him to lead us. Busyness does not mean success. It is just another distraction of the enemy to keep us from following God's plans. We also learned how our growth in the Lord and our steady walk in him was our measuring rod of effectiveness and whether or not we impacted the lives around us. We grew confident that if we allowed the Holy Spirit to daily fill us and be our guide, we would know that he was leading us in the right direction despite obstacles along the way. If we simply trusted in our circumstances, then that would easily lead us incorrectly. This is true because of two reasons. One, the enemy works hard to prevent us from hearing and doing God's plans, and two, God desires faith to come alongside of our obedience.

Being sensitive to the Spirit's leading is vital in serving him. I have a dear friend and sister in Christ whom I met during one of our English corner outreaches. My first impression of her was that she was very outspoken, opinionated, and not a good listener. While all of those things were true about her and while I allowed her loud personality to intimidate me, God had special plans of his own. From the same English corner, I invited a few women to join me in studying the Bible an hour before the English corner was to begin. These women had shown interest in learning more about God.

In our first meeting time, however, my friend with a loud personality showed up early for the weekly English corner and asked us all what we were doing. I explained to her that we were studying the Bible, and she eagerly asked to join in. Still reluctant to befriend her, however, I felt the Holy Spirit led me to welcome her instead.

Her questions about the Word seemed off topic, and she dominated the discussion frequently, leading me to believe she was a distraction for these other women to learn about God. However, one week later she arrived more enthusiastically than before and asked me why God had sent her a stranger to share the gospel with her and her son in the park the other day. She felt it was an answer to my prayers for her and was determined that God was pursuing her. The other women listened intently as she shared with us the gospel tract that was given to her, and she pulled out a new Bible she had purchased for our study time. She then told the other women where they, too, could purchase a Bible. Every week she was the most consistent in coming, and she even pursued the other women to keep coming to our study as well. This woman began changing, and evidence proved that she had made a decision to make Jesus her God. Had I followed my emotions of intimidation with this wonderful sister and friend, I would have missed out on witnessing one of the greatest changes of a person that I have seen in my life, and she would have had to hear the gospel from someone else. We cannot trust our own judgments and emotions as we seek out those called to be God's own. We must trust only the leading of his Spirit.

While working with a married couple who both had years before accepted the Lord, my husband and I felt strongly led by the Holy Spirit to pursue a working partnership with them in ministry. However, when we first approached them, they told us that they could not minister to others. Had God led us in the wrong direction? We had already spent one year of our time investing in our relationship with them and saw much promise in their ability and joy to lead others to Christ and in discipleship. My husband and I returned home from our meeting with them, clearly disappointed and confused, yet we continued to bathe the situation in prayer. With further one-on-one conversations, we learned of their insecurity to serve because of problems they faced in their marriage. They also felt poorly trained and ill-equipped to do so. Soon we realized that the potential we saw in them was not a mistake. They gradually built confidence in their ability to serve after much prayer and counsel from us.

We were planning to host a few summer teams from the States, and we used this opportunity to challenge this local East Asian couple to help us with hosting one of the teams and to offer their home as a meeting place for Bible studies. The purpose was for them to come alongside the team to share the gospel with local university students. One week before those teams arrived, this wonderful East Asian couple finally agreed to help us, and that summer we launched them into a part-time ministry reaching university students. Before too long, their home would become a local house church for these students and a few young professionals invited along the way. My husband and I know that we simply just empowered this couple to take their first steps of faith towards ministry. The rest has been a show of God's greatness and faithfulness as they have with deep conviction opened their home, given their time, and poured their lives out for the local students to know Christ. Only the leading of the Holy Spirit brought this vision to fruit. My husband and I have grown confident that if the Lord leads, he will also equip us with the proper tools and level the obstacles in the way.

Outside of ministry lessons, we also have learned a

great many things. Recognizing more of our human flaws because of the many character issues surfacing while we were on the field, we learned how we were growing more in our dependency of the Lord. In fact, I am thoroughly convinced that God's plan for our lives is for us to first grow more and more dependent on him. It is in our dependency that we have no other choice but to live our lives out of our relationship with him rather than out of our own fallible strength. Anytime I find a way to work out of my own abilities, knowledge, or strength, the Lord creates my circumstances where I cannot succeed without humbly looking to him for help and direction. God wants me to depend on him for every part of my life, and he wants me to trust him with every part of my heart.

On more than one occasion, my husband and I would hear direction from God to do something that we were yet equipped for, and then prior to the plan coming to fruition, God would provide exactly what we needed. We spent much time in prayer, asking him for help in a particular situation that we thought we had under control. As we accepted our life and the reality that we live and serve in a place of uncertainty and instability, we have grown to daily acknowledge our great need for God in order to survive and not be overwhelmed with the high stresses of everyday life. We have grown to be joyfully dependent on his presence in our lives. A day without meeting with God overseas feels like weeks of not hearing his voice. We need him, and we love needing him.

Not only do we have flaws that the Lord allows to surface in us so that he can remove them, but those we serve alongside of are not perfect either. We understood how in a secular workplace we were working with people who lived daily out of their flesh because they did not know the Lord, and our expectations of them were as such. However, when we began to work beside other believers, we dismissed the fact that they, too, can choose to work out of their flesh. This caught us both off guard, and we had to give grace many times to others where we had high expectations of them. They in turn gave us a lot of grace as well. We realized that a mission field in a new land and culture has stripped us all of our comforts, therefore leaving the danger of the worst coming out of us. We saw some continue to grow stronger as believers, and we saw others continue to struggle and grow worse. We rejoiced with those who grew, and we grew sad over those who remained the same or even returned home worse off.

You can never really tell if certain individuals are ready for work overseas. Only the Lord knows what is in their hearts. Those who have thrived alongside of us on the field have been people who were willing to keep teachable spirits. They learned to not isolate themselves in their struggles, instead choosing to be transparent and open with the rest of the team. Anyone can learn a language and a culture, but not everyone can learn to do so hand in hand with the Lord. Today we do not put false expectations on our fellow brothers and sisters anymore. That is unfair to them and us, but we do encourage them and support them when flesh tempts to override faith and obedience. Relaxing our own expectations has made both my husband and I more approachable and better leaders. Our transparency with them has also encouraged them to continue on in perseverance.

We are people who sin, and when we understand that about ourselves and others, we tear down invisible walls of spiritual pride and remove masks that keep us isolated. Not only do we need God, but we also need one another as well. God intends for us to work in unity in his name, always forgiving and holding one another up.

Journal Entry

East Asia
July 30, 2014

I dreamed of our apartment moving up and down. It was an earthquake. An earthquake symbolizes the shaking of one's life foundation. In this dream I saw my local friends, so I knew where I was during the earthquake. I am asking God if this is a literal earthquake or if it is symbolic ... or both. I feel it is more symbolic. This is the fourth dream I have had about earthquakes within the last few months.

Chapter 16

Prophetic Gift

I have yet to share about my growth with the spiritual gifts I received from the Lord. Before I continue, let us remember that just like all believers, there is nothing about me or my personality or my abilities that warrants me worthy of these specific gifts; however, in his grace and sovereignty, God decided to give them to me, and I acknowledge the responsibility of "he who has been given much, much is required." So I often remind myself of these truths in order to keep my heart in check and keep myself humbled.

There are plenty of examples in Scripture where people have not always honored the Lord with what he has given them, and I choose not to be in similar company as those by the grace and mercy of the Lord. I share this to stress the weight I place on glorifying God and not myself. In fact, if I had not been strongly led by God to share these experiences, I would certainly not share them. And believe me—when I share that I first answered the Lord by saying, "I cannot share these vulnerable experiences with so many," he would not relent. If my life is truly not my own, then I can do nothing but obey. And if my testimony proves anything at all, it proves that my life is not special or spectacular, that it remains very ordinary and filled with sin and suffering like so many who are also in much need of God's redemption. No, nothing in me or my life gives reason to why God gave me any gifting or talent at all. He did it for his name alone.

I shared earlier about receiving the gift of seeing into the spirit realm and discerning spirits while touching briefly on my experience with dreams and speaking in tongues. I have not shared about a prophetic gifting. My impression is that I have a strong prophetic gift that encompasses all these other gifts, which explains why I have so many visions and dreams. I did not understand the big picture of a prophetic call on my life until six months ago. I was receiving pieces of the gift throughout my life until I clearly heard the Lord explain to me how he desires to use me with the prophetic. Once he revealed that to me, everything became clear. The intense pruning, the desires in my heart, the pursuit of serving God, and the sorrows I have experienced in life were all part of my preparation to walk responsibly in this gifting. Had this been revealed to me earlier on in my life, I would have surely given this gifting a bad name. I was much too immature and insecure to have understood the proper use of this gift. I am also not saying I am perfect and ready to launch forward full blast in this revelation, but I am at a more mature place in my life and walk with God that I have begun to learn how to fully honor him in walking in this gift.

As I began to piece together my life through the eyes of a servant with a prophetic call, I discovered what I was trying in earnest to figure out most of my life. I discovered what God created me for. Have you ever put together a puzzle and noticed that several pieces were in the wrong spot and you lost the last piece of the puzzle you needed to make it complete? Well, that is how my life was looking until recently. I tried with great determination to find the pieces that would bring my life puzzle together, but I did so in vain. I thought that since I loved to teach the Bible, maybe I was meant to be a Bible teacher. I also thought that since I loved sharing my faith with others, I was meant to be a missionary. Yet I felt something missing as I desired to be used in these ways and more. I was not completely satisfied in these things alone. What was missing was responding to a call that I had missed—a prophetic call.

After the Lord revealed to me this missing puzzle piece, I was still unclear as to what it all meant. I began to study the prophets in Scripture and how God used them to be voices to his people. Then I looked in the New Testament and saw prophecy being used even after Christ had come. God still speaks through this gifting, and I was allowing myself to embrace it as a gift he had given me. I found myself freed up to walk in a powerful way. My lack of knowledge about this gifting kept me from being who God had created me to be. Not being taught or trained in the prophetic gift resulted in my false assumption that true prophets were not here today. And as the Lord directed me to these new and surprising truths, truths that made me aware of who I was in him, I began to grow in fear.

Afraid, I started to realize there was a reason why the prophetic gifting was not taught in my home church. There was also a hidden reason why I had forbidden myself to tell others in my church that I could speak in tongues and see visions. Not everyone in the church receives these truths as scriptural, and after I had attended my university and studied a conservative theology, I was all too aware of the biases against God working in these ways. I came to realize that the person God had created me to be conflicted with the norms and traditions of my church. I felt like a round peg trying to fit in a square hole. But what was I to do? Disobey God in order to please those in the church? Or do

I choose not to fear man, accept how God created me, and fully and passionately obey him? I struggled hard over the revelations God was giving me. I asked myself often why I was not just simply called to be a missionary. Why was this calling so challenging, and why was I struggling so hard to receive it? Then I realized that this struggle started long before this revelation of a prophetic call came. It started the day I made Jesus Lord of my life. This was my struggle with being silenced.

Journal Entry

East Asia
August 1, 2014

So I'm sitting here in Burger King, watching rain pour down hard outside and asking myself several questions. We had a busy summer season with the teams as we expected, and I suffered another bout of illness, which was unexpected. I am thankful that it was not such a crazy summer as it has been prior. Yet I am struggling once again with similar emotions after busy seasons. The emotions feel like burnout topped with culture shock. I feel unappreciated, unsupported, and misjudged. Each time I hit these emotions—or rather they hit me—other emotions come after me as well.

When you're exhausted and down, the enemy attacks. These are the emotions I normally battle with in my life—worthlessness, pain, anger, and confusion. I watch Jordan reach exhaustion as well, but he doesn't have to battle the baggage that I do when I'm tired. I feel like it literally takes me great effort and energy to be a missionary and to live here in East Asia. Each time I go through this, it takes two weeks to get out of it, and I always feel determined we need to go back home. Then I cry a lot. So much pain surfaces in my heart during these times. It's so difficult to get through. But after crying and waiting it out, I feel better. Why do I have this pattern in my life? Sometimes I think I need counseling. God, what do you want me to learn and do in response to these patterns? I feel stuck on this one. I'm at a loss about what to do. If I had more support and was better understood and appreciated, would I be able to battle these things in a healthier way? Do we need to go back to the States so I can get counseling? Is this because of the organization we are a part of? Is this all connected to not being able to conceive? How can I get Jordan to understand what I am going through? Is this an issue of me thinking that the grass is greener on the other side? I think it's a combination of things, and exhaustion brings all of it to the surface.

I'm such a broken person. How can the Lord use me? Why would he want to use me? Do I need a job that is less demanding? Am I insane trying to work such a stress-filled job while battling my past and present issues at the same time? The last dream God gave me filled me with hope as he told me that this grief and my troubles were part of the journey to get me to my destiny. I just need to keep holding on to him and trust him, though I feel like any more grievances in my life will push me to give up all together. Sadly, I have felt this way for five years now. But Jordan discourages me to discuss other options with him, and I feel so alone. Lord, calm the storm within me and help me trust you.

Chapter 17

A Wrong Choice Confronted

God's design for me was not only for me to learn about my specific prophetic gift. He desired to form more of himself in me. In order to do that, he had to pull more of my flesh tendencies out as if he was uprooting bad and rotten roots that were capable of ruining the soil. My husband and I were still in East Asia during the start of the year 2014, and we had learned so much already about ourselves, our ministry, and how to work with others. The lessons that awaited us still would be the toughest I had ever experienced. Thankfully, I started an intense season of journaling everything that God was teaching me, and for an entire year, I poured out my heart on pages that would later benefit me in ways I had no idea.

January was well underway when I started to become increasingly unsatisfied with my life. During this season my husband and I were growing weary of my health issues, the increased busyness of our lives, and the recognition that something was not quite right with me. I knew deep inside that God was certainly trying to get my attention. I found myself feeling confused and questioning my identity when our attempt to have a baby was not so successful. January began with an attempt to get pregnant yet again, but this time we had high hopes that the specialized German doctor we were seeing almost on a weekly basis would be the answer we needed to have a child. Sadly, our efforts were in vain, and the knowledge that the issue had to do with my lack of the right hormones sent me to sit before God, knowing that certainly he had something to say in all of this.

What were layered under heaps of wounds in my heart were some false beliefs that God wanted to change into truths. One of those false beliefs was formed out of a pure disregard to face the truth of my situation. It was easier to believe the lie than to realize the truth. This would not be the first time that I had chosen to believe a lie rather than see my reality and need for change.

In 2011, during our second year of service in East Asia with our organization, my husband and I had attended a meeting for all the missionaries who lived in our part of the world so that we could receive some more training and become better equipped to serve the East Asians. One particular training session that was given blatantly exposed the unspoken beliefs of our organization about the role of women in ministry. Now prior to this event, I had sensed some hints of the inequality of women in this organization, but I was hoping to believe that those beliefs sat with a few people rather than many of my coworkers. I was also hoping that ignoring the hints I saw would serve as an act of humility rather than reacting critically to those red flags. And if that was not enough to get my attention, a year later God put me in a situation where it was more obvious that it was indeed the culture of the organization that encouraged this inequality. It nurtured the belief that the woman could only fill support roles on the mission field and maintain the home while the husband went out to do ministry.

I do have to share here that as I learned more about the

culture of my organization, there were several women I had met who did not come overseas just to support their spouses but to also serve alongside them. I was not surprised to meet both kinds of women, and I do not have any objection or judgment about their reasons for venturing overseas. My hurt stemmed from the small actions that devalued women rather than having a healthy biblical view of us. After I was confronted two different times by two different women about my choice to attend the training session on how to disciple believers rather than the women's class that was being offered, I felt I had done something very wrong. I began growing restless. I did not fit in with the other women because I was not a mother or because I served outside of the home by teaching, training, and preaching alongside my husband. I was becoming more and more disillusioned about the organization we were sent from.

Being told harshly that women should not teach men and feeling overlooked and unappreciated created a deep wound inside of me. I was naive and surprised to find that the biblical issues about women in ministry were still an issue in this day and age. I was even more disturbed that most of the house church leaders we were serving were in fact women themselves because there were no men available to fill those shoes, and they were being trained by some of our missionaries that men should be preaching and pastoring, not them. It saddened my heart deeply.

Another red flag that I chose to ignore was the knowledge that our organization did not encourage specific spiritual gifts found in the Word. This was my greatest objection when my husband and I were making our decision to join this organization or not. The issue brought slight tension in our marriage at the time, and seeking peace, I submitted to my husband's authority and went forward instead of standing on my convictions with joining the organization. Not only did I regret that decision years later, but I also opened myself to new wounds, knowing those red flags were put before me by the Holy Spirit. I essentially ignored God.

The result of my disobedience produced feelings of defeat and great oppression within me. I could not be myself. I could not be who God had created me to be, and because my physical authority limited God and women, my ministry also had limits. All this was deep inside of me, and God wanted me to confront my disobedience, repent, and change. He took me through a season of complete brokenness about what I had done, and I pled with him to set me free from the bondage I had put myself in. I cried out to him to give me the strength and courage to walk out in obedience and to make some choices that I knew would have great consequences for a time but would ultimately bring freedom and change in me. God heard my prayers and comforted me in my brokenness, and then he began to speak.

Journal Entry

East Asia
August 18, 2014

It has been a good three weeks since I have dreamed or journaled anything. These past weeks have been full of brokenness and tears. The Lord helped me recognize why I have been so miserable off and on during our time here in East Asia. The culture of our organization does not fit with who God has made me to be. Yet I took this struggle I had internally with the organization and made it a personal attack against me. The organization is not against me. It is the structure and the spirit of religion and tradition that disagrees with my spirit. Taking away all those hurt emotions, I was able to see my situation with a more level head. I knew from day one that this organization was not what I wanted to be a part of, but I ignored the thoughts, emotions, and red flags that the Holy Spirit revealed to me. I clearly see now how the Lord's hand has been heavy on me because I did not listen to him.

I am now in a state of clear burnout with our work, and it is all my doing. I pushed myself and placed high expectations on both of us to please those in our leadership. I had a lot of anger directed toward our organization, but I was really angry at myself because I had allowed us to come overseas in this way.

I don't think our time here was for nothing. I know in God's grace and mercy, he used our situation to grow me and teach me, which I am utterly thankful for. But now I am ready to make things right. We are leaving East Asia in December, and I pray that God will level the paths for us, showing us clearly where to go and what to do. I pray that in his mercy and kindness, he will give us victory wherever we go just like he did with David. This has not surprised God or thrown his plans out of whack. He knew we would be going through this. My hope and trust is in his faithfulness and sovereignty despite my imperfections and mistakes. God is still in control.

Chapter 18

An Earthquake Coming

I had made a choice that quenched the Holy Spirit in me, though at the time I did not realize I was quenching him. Then I came before him and asked him to forgive me. God responded with much mercy and grace and began to give me dream after dream and vision after vision about what he was about to do in my life.

That I was overwhelmed with how much he was pouring into me would be an understatement. His presence during this season of preparation is unforgettable. I journaled daily and sometimes more than once each day to try to keep up with what he was sharing with me. My dreams were vivid, and the Holy Spirit was clear in helping me interpret them. I began reading more of Scripture, specifically on the prophets, to understand a prophetic gifting. I read books from other women in ministry, devouring their experiences and hoping for an end in this season so that I could bring joy in serving God like they did. I was hoping again.

Then God began giving me warning dreams. He began speaking these same warnings while I would spend time with him in the mornings. Most of the warning dreams had to do with an upcoming earthquake or a shaking foundation, while other dreams had a lot to do with how God saw our organization and what he intended to do with it. I wrote down every dream, every vision, and every word that I heard from him, believing that all would come to pass in his timing. The multiple dreams about earthquakes were God preparing me so that I could endure my own foundation shaking. The dreams about our organization were confirmation of him telling me that he was going to remove us from it.

After three months of God speaking to me on these things and a deep knowing that something was going to happen to shake my foundation, I was full of conflicting emotions. I was excited, anxious, and scared that everything he was sharing with me would happen. Then I began questioning God about what our lives were going to look like beyond that. And I was anxious for it to happen sooner than it would. Daily, I read through the things he showed me in my journals so that I would not forget what he had promised me. I continued to journal as I waited for him to move, not knowing what that move was going to be. I waited and trusted and held onto him.

Journal Entry

East Asia
September 9, 2014

Dear Heavenly Father,

I am experiencing much grief, anger, and depression. But today I feel your mercy over me despite all of these emotions, making me desperate and hungry for more of you. So along with my prayers for healing and help to forgive myself and others, I am now going to ask for more of you.

I need to shut out the voice of the enemy in my life. Help me to keep him out. I give you, Holy Spirit, access to my dreams, only you and not the enemy. I shut him out in the name of Jesus. I will not, by God's mercy, allow this world to corrupt me or change me. I will not allow the enemy to gain a foothold on me because of my pain. I choose to trust in you, Lord, not in this world or in myself. Keep me from slipping, Lord. Protect me from myself, and hold onto me, Heavenly Father.

Chapter 19

A Dream Comes True

One night I had a very powerful and vivid dream that showed me destruction in the country we were living in. I could not tell what had been the cause of all these things, but I guessed that it was a natural disaster or something on that level. I knew it was not an earthquake because I walked onto the scene in my dream after the chaos had already happened, and I had not felt an earthquake in the dream. One building in my dream had shattered glass everywhere at the base of it. Buildings were damaged nearby too, and debris covered the streets. I immediately looked for Jordan and realized that he was out of town, so I called him. He calmed me down and said that he was safe, and then he told me to get to a safe place. Then I woke up.

After waking up, I went over the dream in my mind again and again, trying to make sense of it, and suddenly, I remembered that Jordan was due to take a trip out of town one week later. I wrote down the dream and prayed and felt a deep peace that we both would be okay. I had felt that in the dream, but I still could not keep myself from sharing all of this with Jordan. His trip was scheduled for the beginning of August, and he would be gone for ten full days, the longest we had both been apart from one another. Neither of us looked forward to that time of separation. We had just finished a busy summer full of hosting teams for two long months and had done a few trainings as well that took great energy from us. This planned trip was coming on the tail end of a busy summer, and at this time I was personally exhausted.

Why we had scheduled more activity after a busy summer I cannot remember specifically, though I am confident that we were trying too hard to please our supervisor by providing more opportunities to train our local brothers and sisters. Jordan's trip was one of those opportunities, and though our intentions were good, the timing was just very challenging.

I looked forward to ten days of staying home, resting, and putting our home back in order after ignoring necessary chores because of the busyness of the summer. What I did not look forward to was feeling lonely without Jordan, so I intended to meet up with some very good friends during that long week. By the time Jordan was away, I had already put my dream I had had a week prior to bed. I did not know for sure if anything would take place while Jordan was gone, but I believed it was possible something would happen spiritually.

Well, I happened to be only half correct about that assumption. Jordan was gone no longer than twenty-four hours before the news showed an enormous gas explosion that occurred in a neighborhood in a nearby country. The explosion was a result of a huge gas leak in the pipes traveling underneath a busy road and residential area. I saw this on television, and with much horror, I saw footage of the explosion after a man had taped it with his phone. In the footage you can see an explosion begin and continue down the road, turning the street inside out with cars and people becoming its victims. Windows shattered from the impact of the explosion, and many witnesses at first thought they were experiencing a huge earthquake. The explosions continued on for quite a distance, maybe about half a mile, and from a view of a high apartment window, it looked like the neighborhood was being bombed repeatedly. It was destruction and chaos. I cried, watching the news anchor share the death toll, and I immediately called Jordan. He had not yet heard the news where he was, but he was also saddened.

Two days later another explosion quite closer to our city occurred in a factory full of workers. This, too, was a devastating event, and it felt overwhelming, especially after the last explosion. Many factories in East Asia do not follow the rules and safety regulations, and many of these factories have horrible records because of their lack of safety. The news in East Asia does not hold back either. Correspondents show gruesome images on our television screens, something that often kept me from watching the news. However, after a friend told me about the nearby explosion, I braved the television for more information. Of course, it was just as heartbreaking.

As the week continued and with Jordan's absence, I was becoming more aware of my exhaustion from the summer and my developing health issues. Watching all of the real-life devastation on television did not help either. My mental and emotional health was beginning to give way. Every night I battled strong emotions of great sadness, grief, and anxiety because I was working in another country under the authority of our organization. I cried a lot that week. This was the start of many tears soon to follow.

However, I met with a new friend toward the end of that week who had shared some of her story and background with me. Years ago she had been a part of our same organization, and now she and her husband had returned overseas with a different organization. Her intention was not to convince me to leave our organization. On the contrary, she was sharing just tidbits of her experiences in East Asia and how God had brought her to a place where she could serve him with the freedom from her struggles with depression. I listened intently because I knew I was currently fighting depression and I knew the appointment with her was a divine one from God. She ended our time together by praying over me, and the words the Holy Spirit put in her heart sounded as if Jesus himself was praying over me. She did not know my silent struggle at all. I chose not to tell her at that time, but her powerful prayer and the word she spoke over me were exactly what I needed to hear. After praying, she prophetically told me to do what was in my heart to do. That was it. Those simple words cut through my hurt and pain and stirred activity within me. On my way home, I made a much-needed decision. I decided that it was time to return to the States to pursue a deeper calling in my life. I just had to wait for God to speak the same thing to Jordan.

The horrific events that took place the weekend prior to God speaking clearly to me paralleled the turbulent emotions that produced so much chaos within me. God giving me new direction did not bring calmness to my soul but rather sparked a further explosion that was meant to shake my very foundation.

Journal Entry

East Asia
September 23, 2014

Lots of things to write about! Depression has really gotten a hold on me this year, especially during these last two months. I got a hold of a book, which definitely fell into my hands by divine workings, and it has revealed to me the open door in my heart where depression has found its way in to take hold of me. As I was reading this book—and I'm still working my way through it—my anxiety would begin to surface. That surprised me yet also showed me where the root of my depression came from.

Though I'm still reading the book and processing what I am reading, it has started an awareness of what is going on in my complex heart. And our hearts are very complex! I was talking with Jordan about some of what I read, and I saw a vision in my mind. I saw myself as a seven-year-old, maybe younger, and the Lord showed me how I had put her behind a locked door in order to protect her. I haven't let her out since. That part of me who the girl represents is me as a child. I took on being an adult at a young age in order to survive life because not all of my needs were being met as a child. But you can only lock that child up for so long because she needs to be let out and nurtured and brought back to the adult part, making the person whole and complete.

The pain I have been experiencing comes from that child part of me that hasn't been allowed to cry or feel angry or be a child at all. In his mercy and grace, the Lord has used my current situation overseas to put me in a place of weakness so that I can deal with this pain. He has allowed infertility issues, trouble with our organization, the complexities of living in a difficult culture and place, and my ongoing burden of trying to please my parents and any authority above me to bring me to more brokenness. I never imagined I needed to be broken again, but here I am broken beyond belief, sitting before the Father, asking him to put the pieces back together again as he sees fit.

I had dealt with my father issues several years back, and that delivered me from depression then. But now confronting my mother and stepfather issues has truly been painful and difficult as they have a stronger hold on me. The night the Lord revealed to me that I needed to let the little Tabitha out of the locked room and allow him to heal her, I had a dream in which I was being delivered from a stronghold. The Holy Spirit spoke through me as I was commanding the enemy to leave me. In my awareness of this God-given revelation, I have begun deliverance of the enemy and the pain.

I want to say that I am completely better, but I know that time will continue to reveal what I need to deal with, and healing will come as I become whole before the Lord and by the Lord. My question for God now is how to move forward with this revelation. The Lord is so kind and patient with me, and I need to be patient with myself as I heal.

Chapter 20

Foundation Shaking

The health issues that I had been battling up to this point began when Jordan and I first tried to start a family three years prior. My first early miscarriage was followed by an unfortunate electric bike accident and then unexplained bouts of physical exhaustion and stomach pains that prompted multiple doctor visits, exams, and blood testing. All of this eventually led to a discovery that I possibly had a benign tumor located on my pituitary gland in my brain. An MRI confirmed the diagnosis. I had to undergo four months of strong medicine to shrink the tumor, and I desperately cried out to God to heal me. He brought the miracle I was seeking and healed me of the tumor.

Once the tumor was gone, Jordan and I decided to try again to have a child. We eventually visited a wonderful German doctor in Shanghai to see if she could help us since we had again endured two more early miscarriages. However, after traveling back and forth from our city to a neighboring city to see the doctor, we only learned more about why we were having infertility problems. Other than that, we experienced yet another early miscarriage. The summer we just had with the university teams and all its energy-draining activities clearly affected our infertility problems. I had had my fifth early miscarriage over the span of three years while the teams were with us. This time, however, we did not plan to try to get pregnant. In fact, we had made a decision to stop trying for a season so that my health would improve and my hormones would balance out. Having another early miscarriage definitely brought me to a place of more brokenness. I needed to know what God wanted for us in this life and why he was allowing so much heartache.

After I decided in my heart that it was time to return back to the States and after I shared this with my husband, he understood why I had made this choice, knowing everything that I had personally been dealing with. But he still wanted to hear from the Lord about such a life-changing decision. So I also waited on the Lord with Jordan. However, the waiting agitated my depression and my anxiety. Weeks continued to pass, and the depression would not ease. In fact, I felt myself growing worse every day, and my anxiety prevented me from sleeping well at night. I had months earlier signed up for an online university course to enhance my ability to serve the East Asians with a new platform idea, but the week prior to the class beginning, I panicked and pulled out, hoping we would be reimbursed. After this action, Jordan could clearly see something was indeed wrong with me.

I would have never backed out of anything that I was committed to before, and how I panicked opened his eyes to my dire situation. By the third week, Jordan and I recognized that my depression was becoming a greater problem than either of us could deal with. By this time, all activity outside of the home for me had almost ceased. I would feel a sadness deep within me overwhelm me, and then I would go into our bedroom and cry. I was losing hope for our future, and I had no idea why this depth of depression was even troubling me.

I was confused and alone, and I felt all the guilt in the world for dragging my husband through all this with me. Within one month I felt my world falling to pieces, and I could not tell you why. All I could do was pray to God to let me return back to the States or take me home to be with him.

One night while Jordan and I were taking one of our numerous walks we had during difficult times, I shared with him a picture of how I was feeling. I told him that I was falling down a huge dark pit, grasping for anything that I could, and I was becoming unsuccessful at my attempts. I felt I was just free-falling deeper inside of this pit. This description saddened Jordan deeply, and together, we shared our tears. Not only was my foundation being shaken, but Jordan's was as well. He wanted to help me, but at this point, he did not know how. However, this was just the beginning.

Journal Entry

The States
December 27, 2014

And David became more and more powerful, because the Lord Almighty was with him.

—1 Chronicles 11:9 (NIV)

Clearly, I am in a battle, and I've been fighting these same demons for years. I allowed their lies to confuse me and torment me, but as I hold onto the truths that God has revealed to me over this past year, truths of the dysfunction of my family, truths of his Word, I am able to recognize the lies. The enemy hates this so much. I know because he has been attacking me in my sleep and trying desperately to get me to believe those lies again through my dreams. But I wake up, and out loud, I reject the bad dreams and the lies. This season of healing will also be a time for God to strengthen and empower me as I seek him in this. Lord, empower me like you did David, who also ran for his life. Amen!

Chapter 21

Painful Decisions

My husband and I both strongly desired to serve overseas. We both felt a call to reach the unreached for the gospel, and we had committed our lives to serve overseas for as long as the Lord allowed. So when we had to make a decision whether or not to return home from service overseas, we fell into a time of grieving and testing. Knowing other missionaries on the field and having strong friendships with them made us fully aware that we were not the only ones who doubted the call to live and serve overseas. By this time, Jordan and I had been down this road of questioning whether or not it was time to return home more than once, but this time the road seemed to darken and lengthen as I struggled. My emotional and mental health was definitely on the line for this decision, and we knew deep within us that God's sovereignty of allowing these struggles would not be met with stubbornness on our part. We were willing to receive what God wanted for us both, even if it meant an entire uprooting of our lives from East Asia.

I am an avid runner. I enjoy running for the pleasure of it as well as the stress relief. One night in July, a month before I really made a decision to return home, I was out on a run, and I began asking God some serious questions as I tried to process the early miscarriage I just had. I suddenly stopped during the run and literally cried out to God, asking him what he wanted from me in all of this suffering, and in angst I asked him if he was trying to get me to return to the States. As soon as those words left my mouth, I knew that God had indeed answered me. He was bringing our call full circle and positioning us to go back to our own home culture. This pivotal night was the start of me receiving into my heart the reality of us possibly returning home. For Jordan it was a different process. His was watching me and how I was responding to the culture, our work, and him. He witnessed me go from embracing and loving the culture to having panic attacks from trying simply to cross the road. His concern for me and my well-being was his leading us to return home.

We had an upcoming visa trip out of country scheduled for us at the beginning of September, and we had decided that we would make our final decision on that trip whether to return home for good or keep pressing on with the hopes that I would get better in time. Of course, we struggled on this trip and became anxious with the thought that if we did move in this new direction, we would have to inform our supervisors, our teammates, our families, and all of our supporters. There would be many disappointed parties who had invested in training and supporting us if they learned we were moving back home. We had to hear from God clearly— that was for sure.

We made our final decision on that trip, and we prepared ourselves to first meet with our supervisors to inform them of my depression and our decision to resign. They welcomed our decision with all the grace and wisdom that we needed and thus began a new journey for our lives. We had thought that making the decision was the most challenging part of all this, but we came to find out that it was only the push over the waterfall. We still had the falling part to endure. During the next couple of months, our marriage was tested with much grief, sorrowful good-byes, meetings with counselors, and learning that we both had placed our self-worth in our job as missionaries above being children of God.

Fear took hold of us each time we had to explain our reasons for leaving the field, telling a local brother or sister, a family member, or another coworker. We feared being judged and being misunderstood. We feared disappointing people. We eventually learned that these fears gripped our hearts because we valued too highly the approval and acceptance of others rather than God. This was definitely a life-changing lesson as we allowed ourselves to let go of these fears and began placing our self-worth in being God's children. The importance of this lesson would carry us throughout returning home and rebuilding our lives as we had to make the right decisions for ourselves rather than continuing to please others.

Grieving a lifelong dream was at times unbearable for me. I was faced with a false guilt almost daily. I felt I was taking my husband away from a life he enjoyed and loved, and I was also battling the lies that I had failed God. Even though I was confident that God was the one orchestrating this life change, I still had an enemy that would rather discourage me with a lie. All of my emotions during this time felt like they were attacking me. One day I would face fear. The next I would be faced with guilt, and leaving behind all of our dear local brothers and sisters tightened my throat and brought many tears to my eyes. It was enough having to already deal with depression and anxiety, but all of these new emotions that naturally came with such a huge transition from a career of service left me exhausted and unmotivated to get anything done. My daily routine grew simpler and simpler as my energy lessened, but I chose to remain hopeful that one day the darkness would have to fade. After all, the sun had always risen after a long night. My hope was still in God, though it was a faint hope. It was time to allow him to give me a new dream for my life.

Journal Entry

The States
January 2, 2015

I have much to be thankful for right now. I am thankful that God revealed to me the truth about my parents. I was talking with Jordan about how I was feeling after I accepted and recognized that reality. I shared how it felt like a bag had been over my head for so many years; however, now the bag had finally been removed, and I am able to see for the first time the truth about the unhealthy relationship with my parents. A whole bunch of emotion has been stirred in me! I am relieved to know the truth. I am in sorrow and grief about it all. I am angry, and I am deeply depressed. *But ...* I am thankful to know the answer to the many questions I have had since I was a child.

I feel like a new person, and at the same time, I feel that my life has been wasted under that bag of lies. If I had known this truth before, I am certain I would have hurt myself. God knew the right time to reveal it to me. And I am thankful for his wisdom. Lord, I am thankful to see the reality of what I was living under, and I am thankful you removed and delivered me from all the lies. I ask you, Lord, to help me keep that bag off my head. I can see how two years ago you were preparing me for this revelation, and though I grieved at the time, I still refused to take the bag off fully. I was scared to accept my reality because it was too painful to deal with. Yet you love me so much that you would not let me ignore my pain.

Because I had not dealt with it, my pain grew into an infection, and that affected all the parts of my life. We left East Asia because I knew that I needed to face my pain and my reality. I am ready Lord to go through the healing process with you. I truly am thankful that you did not let me grow worse, that you kept allowing the pain to surface, and that you insisted in a gentle way that I remove the bag. Help me to remain thankful. Help me to heal. Help me seek your face always in this.

Chapter 22

My Darkest Pit

Before I received that dream, however, I had to first learn some truths about my life. Being painfully aware that I was struggling with depression and anxiety on deeper levels than before in my life stirred within me questions of where this was coming from and why. I naively believed that I had dealt with all my baggage from my past—my sins, the loss of my biological father from my life, and some painful memories during my childhood. Yet here I was battling depression again, and I had no idea where it was coming from. I was growing afraid that I was just literally going crazy and that there was something terribly wrong with the chemicals in my brain. I thought also perhaps my tumor had returned, but in a more horrible way, affecting more than one hormone.

I am a firm believer that the enemy cannot come in and bring on an illness without finding an open door, and I was aware that this persistent sadness was a sign of illness—mental and emotional illness. Whether I was facing a spiritual attack or had opened a door for him through my own choices of sin, an unseen wound within me, or a generational curse, I knew that I needed to seek God on this one. He would know, and he had always been faithful to me before to reveal to me the spiritual side of my situation.

As Jordan and I were going through a big collection of books in our office in order to downsize before our move back to the States, I ran across a book about mothers. It was a book written to inform and help adults heal from their childhood as a result of some dysfunctional parenting from their mother. I read the back cover and the description of the book, thought about putting it in the giveaway pile when I found myself only moments later picking it back up again and reading the first chapter. I had no real reason to find fault in the way my mother parented me. I knew her life circumstances when she married my father and then later my stepfather, and I was aware that these circumstances would bring challenges to her parenting skills, but I had confidence that how I was parented was not the source of my current struggles.

And yet I continued to read on and found myself struggling more with anxiety as I read. While I was reading the book, there were moments when I found I identified with the testimonies in it, and I would run to the bathroom to cry with a panic attack coming over me. The book was not the source of the panic attacks, but its contents through testimonials were. I found the book to be very helpful in moving forward in forgiveness and in life, but I questioned the panic attacks. What was happening was that my head had accepted and dealt with some difficult issues from my past, but my heart and my soul had yet healed from them. The anxious reaction was coming from deep within me, a physical symptom of a deeper wound left open and vulnerable. My depression was also a symptom of a deeper wound. The Lord had revealed to me so much already, and he would show me more still.

Once my husband and I had already shared with our supervisors about our decision to return back to the States, it was time to share with our families. Then we had to decide where to live once we left, and we made that decision wisely. I had had some issues with my mother in my past, and I wanted to keep clear from anything that would bring on more stress than I was able to handle, which was not much. Patterns in my previous relationship with my parents revealed an obvious dysfunction. It was clear they perceived me not as an adult but still as a very submissive child. This perception was unchanged because I had only challenged it a handful of times throughout my young adult life. So when my husband and I shared with my parents that we had decided to live closer to Jordan's parents for this season of our lives, there was obvious anger on the other end of the phone line. The conversation was cut short by my mother, and I was left confused and hurt. Little did I know at the time how that would be the last conversation I would have with both my parents for a really long time, and how it would start unraveling my reality. A reality I had to face and deal with in order for healing to take place.

My parents refused to connect with me for weeks after that phone call, and I was not so eager to connect with them either. Great emotions had risen within me when my mother treated my husband and me the way she did. A flood of memories about how she and I interacted during similar confrontations came to the forefront of my mind. All of those instances had occurred after I had already left for college. I was an adult by then. Our relationship had no hard edges when I was a child and a teen. I never challenged my parents' authority in my life, but I always submitted and kept to the rules of the house. It was only when I had moved off to attend school that our relationship began its rocky ride, and since then nothing really had changed—nothing except I was growing more and more weary of being mistreated and my mother was growing in fear that she could not control me as before.

With all of these memories and emotions at the forefront of my mind, my depression and anxiety grew worse. I would find myself in my bathroom or my bedroom, sitting alone and crying out to the Lord to take my life. I begged him to either move in my situation with my parents once and for all or remove me from this world. My despair was growing worse with these horrible thoughts, and still, we had another month to endure before heading back to the States. As each day grew closer to our departure, I often panicked, thinking I would have to deal with this conflict again, and I did not know what to do. I could not endure East Asia anymore, and now I did not want to return home. Where could I go to be safe?

Journal Entry

The States
January 4, 2015

Lord, I grow stronger each day. Though this revelation has brought me more pain than I have ever experienced in my life, accepting the truth has also brought me a new hope and peace. Now knowing that I have been living a guilt- and shame-based life as a result of continual verbal and emotional abuse against me as an adult child allows me to see the problem and also identify its root cause. This knowledge has given me clarity and understanding in how to move forward with my healing. This I am thankful for, and knowing that you, God, have always been with me comforts me. I want to help others recognize and be set free from their abuse. I do not want my pain and struggles to have been in vain. Continue to use my life for your glory, Lord.

Chapter 23

Breaking a Pattern

The Lord wanted me to see that the issue of my depression and anxiety was indeed paralleled with my relationship with my parents. I was aware of a horrible pattern that had formed in my life. I would make a life-changing decision, and my mother would disagree with this decision because she would have chosen otherwise. She would convince my stepfather that I was in error, and then after her confronting me, I would be mistreated and punished with no contact from them until I found the error of my ways. Eventually, I would ask for their forgiveness and change my decision so that it aligned with theirs. Like I said before, it was an awful pattern in the relationship I had with my parents during my young adult years.

Being treated like this over years becomes wearisome. My personal response to being rejected by my parents and living under rules of conditional love instead of unconditional love more than likely put me in a low state of mind so that I subconsciously related their rejection with a rejection from the Lord. I had a difficult time separating my relationship with God and the relationship I had with my parents. I often caved into their wishes and would try harder the next time to please my parents but with little to no avail. Of course, God saw this pattern as well, and he was moving in ways where the pattern would need to come to an end in order for me to move forward in life with him.

It takes an awful lot of courage to end an unhealthy pattern in an important relationship. It also takes an awful lot of needing to know your identity is in Christ. When we are securely rooted in God we are able to face the rejection that can come when we put up boundaries and choose change. For me it took two years of preparation from God before I could take this kind of stand. My thinking needed to change concerning God, me, all authority in my life, and my parents. God intended to uproot false beliefs that were holding me back from learning some important truths about my inner being. Of course, this would take time.

Two years prior to me taking my stand with my mother, God was revealing to me—and had been for years—the unhealthy parts of our relationship. But he was specifically answering an old prayer. I had asked him repeatedly what the cause of my mother's wrong behavior was. I had believed it to be something real, but I could not put words to identify her behavior. I could not put words to how my mother's behavior toward me made me feel. I came to learn about personality disorders on a talk show. The daughters of a certain family were confronting their mother who had a narcissistic personality disorder. Their testimonies of how they felt under their mother's control, jealousy, and manipulation piqued my interest. I wanted to understand narcissism more. I did my own research on the Internet. I read definitions, descriptions, tests, and multiple testimonies of the victims of narcissists, and I broke. I knew the Lord wanted me to be able to understand the bondage my mother was in. I was willing to accept depression or anger issues, but what I was reading was very difficult to accept. I kneeled before the Lord that night, crying out to him in pain and asking him to help me understand and process all that I was learning. I could easily relate to almost all of the testimonies I had read, and I felt that there were other people out there who understood what I had been under for years; however, I was still not able to accept it completely. I told the Lord I was not ready to confront this problem, and so I put away all that I had read and felt.

Two years later it all surfaced again, but this time I knew that I had to confront my situation and that ignoring it or keeping my mother happy was not the answer anymore. My relationship with her was not real. I never gave an honest answer to her questions. I knew what she wanted to hear and what would keep her off my back, and that is how I answered her. In short, I was being a *good child* in order to keep the peace with her and my stepfather. It became painfully clear that I could not share with her certain parts of my life that I knew she would not receive well. She did not like hearing that I was having infertility issues, and she was unable to bring real comfort to our conversations, so I began to only share with her the good things that were happening in my life. But when we decided that the best place for us to live was my husband's hometown during our season of transition back into the States, she made it very clear that she did not like our decision. She did not try to understand our decision, and her focus was not on me needing to heal from depression but rather on her having her way. I was very hurt.

During the six weeks that we did not communicate, I realized that I needed a change, or I would only grow worse. I was exhausted from everything that was going on in our lives—the move back to the States, the realization of a career change hitting hard, and dealing with a real illness. I asked God repeatedly what to do. I was afraid to see my mother, afraid of her rejection and disapproval, and afraid of her anger and the high possibility of her confronting me. I was afraid of her to call me, and I was afraid that I would not be able to handle life anymore with her as an enemy rather than a mother. All these fears I placed before the Lord, asking him to strengthen me, to give me courage, and to help me.

When it was time for Jordan and I to fly back to the States, we decided to head straight to his hometown to give ourselves time to rest and begin our adjustment back home. We still had not heard from my parents even after we had e-mailed them of our flight departures from East Asia and our arrival into LA. They were obviously still angry with our decision. The week after arriving, I had time to really think and pray about how to respond to my mother's behavior. I cried out to God, and he answered me. He showed me the lives of others in Scripture who had been separated from their families for seasons, specifically Joseph and David in the Old Testament. He showed me Jesus's words about putting a rightful boundary up with his own mother and brothers when he was preaching the Word. God clearly spoke to me. I knew already the problem and the answer, and I needed to trust my own judgment now. He had prepared me to face my problems and not ignore them or run away from them. So I decided to write my mother a heartfelt letter because I was still too scared of her to tell her in person or over a phone call. I told her that during this season of healing, I needed to make some personal changes to my life and that I needed to stop our relationship for now until I had made those changes.

I knew that I needed space for my sanity and health. I knew that I could not be put through another pattern that would lead me down an even darker path. I knew that I needed time to renew my mind. I knew that I needed to put a stop to my mother's hurtful behavior and finally be someone who told her no. Do I believe that she actually has a personality disorder? I am not a psychiatrist or a clinical counselor, so I cannot (and will not) label her with one, but I do know that the manipulation, control by fear, and emotional and verbal abuse needed to stop. So I made a brave and difficult decision to not receive it anymore.

Journal Entry

The States
January 6, 2015

The Lord has chosen me to walk through this. He has chosen me to be raised by my parents, to be in a dysfunctional environment, and to stand up against the abuse and threats. He chose me to understand victims of hurt parents. He believed I would keep my eyes on him throughout the years of abuse and great confusion. He believed I was able to come through it stronger with him. He has used these years of abuse as the tool to mold me more into his likeness. He used East Asia to make me aware of why I battled depression and to position me to walk away from the abuse. The abusive relationship was my well, my prison, my lion's den to keep me dependent on God and not on my own strength. He has chosen me to walk this valley for his glory and my growth. Now it is time to walk out of the valley.

Chapter 24

Renewing My Mind

As I allowed the Lord to reveal to me the false beliefs I was living with and the hurt that needed healing, I was not unaware that I would need to replace those false beliefs with truths. I needed an overhaul on my mind, and I needed to have the mind of Christ more than ever if I wanted to be healed of depression and anxiety. I have allowed the Lord before to renew my thinking, and I wholeheartedly believe that it is a lifelong process to gain a renewed mind in God. I was definitely at a new stage in life where the renewal process needed to reach deeper within my being.

I had already made the difficult and sometimes overwhelming decision to break away from my mother for this season of healing, which also naturally affected the relationships I had with my entire family, and I had made this decision prior to seeing a clinical counselor. Once meeting with the counselor and learning differences between functional and dysfunctional families, I knew the decision I made to separate from my parents was the healthiest thing for me, and I was gaining a better understanding of why the Lord had led me to make such a choice. Before sending my mother that letter, I weighed the costs and the risks very heavily and at the beginning battled false feelings of guilt, condemnation, and self-hatred. A battle waged on within my mind for months after making the separation, and at times I thought I would not be able to make any improvements. I continued to see the counselor and shared with her the little progress I had made, and she celebrated with me that I was in fact getting better.

I finally allowed myself to grieve at this time. I grieved more about having to return from the mission field. I grieved not being able to see my parents. I grieved about coming out of an abusive relationship where emotional and verbal abuse had been my norm, and I grieved that in my thirties I had to relearn who I was. The interesting part of all of this was how I was able to clearly see and recognize the mistreatment the longer I was out of it. I was allowing myself to see it instead of push it down or ignore it. I grew stronger in my decision each day to keep away from my parents, and I grew to understand God's true character apart from them. The latter was the most important lesson that I had gained.

On a daily basis, I would tell myself that God loved me unconditionally and that if I made a mistake, I would choose to still receive his love. I told myself each morning that leaving an unhealthy relationship behind would give room for me to heal, blossom, and grow. I would take thoughts of despair or negativity captive and change them to what God says about me in his Word. I spent time in prayer and Bible reading every day despite my fluctuating emotions. I began an exercise routine and changed my eating habits to improve my health as well, and slowly but surely, I found that I was being put back together again under God's hand. It was an amazing and very trying time for me.

As I waged war against the lies I had believed for most of my life, lies that the enemy had cunningly hidden deep within me, those who knew me well could actually see a physical change in my appearance. I was happy. I had not lost all hope, and God's great faithfulness in my life had proven to be real. I was becoming stronger in my ability to recognize the enemy's lies when they were whispered in my ear, and I was growing confident in my identity as God's daughter. I saw the light at the end of the tunnel. I knew that this winter season would indeed end and that spring would take its course. The enemy could no longer use my own family to try to destroy me. I had a choice to say no and to allow God to protect me by removing the chains that held me in slavery. I had been freed when Christ won his victory on the cross, but now it was time to live in that freedom and not be afraid anymore.

Journal Entry

The States
January 10, 2015

God, I have to be honest. Even though I know the truth about my family's dysfunctional ways and I know the truth of your Word, I still struggle with guilt. It's like a cycle I go through. I will feel the guilt and then rebuke the enemy. Then I will feel the shame and then rebuke the enemy. Then I become insecure, and I have to read what your Word says about me again. Then when I feel you within me, I feel on top of the world and that my struggles are over. Then a new day comes, and I have to start all over again, training my thoughts to align with your truth. I have to remind myself every day that I am free and you love me unconditionally. It's not easy, Lord. I make you my stronghold in this season of my life.

Chapter 25

Deep Within

God was changing me from deep within, and to do so, he purposefully led me into a storm. I willingly allowed him to do so as he had prepared me beforehand. However, I was unaware of how deep the Lord would allow me to go in this valley. I had been through several valleys in my life, but I cannot say that any of them have come close to the pain and anguish of this valley. But for God to uproot the things in my life that were not bringing him glory or helping me in any way, I had to walk through this valley. Somewhere deep within me, I knew that I needed to face this valley one day. I knew that I needed God to uproot some nasty things in order to become more like Christ, but I was hoping that it would just be uprooted in an easier way.

If you know anything about digging up roots as my husband who studied horticulture does, the process is tough, messy, and at times extremely frustrating. Some roots have grown so deep that they are extremely difficult to dig out. Sadly, the same goes with people. How can you bear good fruit if you have a bad root planted within you? You have a hard time trying to control all the bad fruit that wants to grow, and more energy is used up in the process, so the good fruit somehow comes through by the grace of God alone. Would not it be better to have all our energy focused not on trying to prevent bad fruit from growing but on reaping good fruit? What a life we could live like that!

After receiving much healing and allowing the Lord to renew my mind, I was starting to hear him put a new call within my heart. In order for me to live without shame, I set my mind and heart toward a hope that God would use my story to help others find their freedom and joy in him. I did not want any of my struggles to have been in vain, and so I told the Lord to use all that I went through and experienced for him. I wanted others to experience the freedom I now had and the awareness that they had a choice to not live under abuse either.

The Lord heard my prayer, and through another woman's testimony, my passion to serve the Lord was reignited. My husband and I had served in full-time ministry for five years together, and we had our ups and downs. But with me battling health issues and depression overseas, I became exhausted and apprehensive about serving God again. I just did not trust that I could serve him and remain healthy. I was discouraged, burned out, and tired. I had many doubts, and I specifically asked how God could use me again. However, after hearing this woman share her testimony about God calling her to be a lioness for him and going out and fighting so that the lost could know him and be delivered from the enemy, something inside of me broke. I began crying and cried for more than an hour as the Holy Spirit came deep within me and healed me from all the pain and hurt I had received while serving overseas. I then began confessing to the Lord how I wanted him to still use me to gather the lost and bring them to him. I wanted people to know God still, and I wanted to be used by him. The week following my cry,

I gained more energy and vision for the future than I had in a really long time, and I began to allow myself to dream again.

I searched out three women who had started their own ministries and asked if I could interview them and learn from them. All were eager to help me and pour into me their own experiences and calls to ministry. Each interview I did, I grew in purpose and excitement. The Holy Spirit was definitely stirring within me a new call to start my own ministry in order to reach others. He provided mentors to give me direction and wisdom. He reignited a long-lost dream I had to be a speaker and author, and he strengthened me to follow through with it all. Most importantly, God revealed to me that East Asia was not the only ministry he had for me but that it was part of the process of preparing me for something new, for something I was created specifically to do.

Journal Entry

The States
January 19, 2015

Heavenly Father, something happened to me last night as I was watching the testimony of a woman on a television show. She was sharing how God was awakening the lioness within her, the lioness attributes he put inside of her to serve him. I then began to cry uncontrollably. I felt the Holy Spirit inside of me, speaking to me. I was crying because that dream was also my heart's true desire. I wanted to be awakened in order to serve you, Lord, in a new and powerful way.

Father, thank you for showing me and awakening in me the desires you put in my heart. I was talking with my best friend about the experience, and after I explained that my crying was definitely a healing as well as an awakening, she told me that the healing was taking place in my inner soul. Her explanation and words clicked with me. I've only cried maybe twice since being back from overseas, and both times were over my parents. This cry was about a deep desire within me to continue serving the Lord and a grieving over leaving East Asia. It was an awakening of my soul, my spirit, and I would move forward with the dreams you had put into me a long time ago. The seed you planted in me is sprouting quickly.

Chapter 26

Silenced No More

I have been waiting to write this chapter with great anticipation and not because it happens to be the last chapter of this book. Now I am able to confidently put in words and vocalize that I am no longer under the thumb of the enemy. I am no longer silent. I have a greater understanding of God's character and love. I recognize how God's sovereignty is very real and powerful in my life. I am able to clearly see as I look back over my life and specifically this past year how the Lord orchestrated each experience and struggle I went through in order to bring me more character growth, self-awareness, and healing. Yet the most exciting part of these experiences is seeing what the enemy chose to use to try to destroy me and how God Almighty used those attempts of the enemy to build in me a story that is unique in its own.

I used the Word of God to carry me through my most trying times and found out how many figures in the Bible that God used to show his glory and character had stories of their own. Reading their stories that involved suffering, pain, and valleys gave me confidence that God was doing the same with me. In many of my prayers during this season and afterward, I asked God to use my valley experiences to help others walk through theirs. I did not want to have experienced my struggles and battles in vain. I wanted to keep bringing glory to God, and I wanted to be used by God to help others.

One of those biblical characters that strengthened me through his life story was King David. He had an intimate relationship with God as a shepherd overlooked in his large family, yet he was chosen by God to sit on a king's seat, leading the Israelites. Prior to him stepping into his destiny David's life consisted of trial after trial. The devil did not want him to succeed and become king. In fact, he was trying awfully hard to ruin David's reputation and get him killed. However, we clearly see how God used these trials and events to shape David into the man that God had destined him to become. This is God's sovereignty at work, and we are able to see it as we pull back and look over David's entire life. If David's story had ended right after he was anointed by Solomon, then it would not have brought much glory to the Lord and perhaps might not have found its lengthy place in the Bible. But we see that God followed through with his promise to David in a powerful way, and I truly believe David held onto that promise with all his might as he ran for his life. David held onto hope because the Lord gave him hope to hold onto. God had a plan for David, and David believed God in that plan.

I strongly believe that was how I was able to press on through in the darkest times of my life. I knew that each valley had to end, and God's promises in his Word became my hope for my life. I am not saying it was easy, but I am saying that I was never alone in those dark times. I heard something the other day that put words to how I felt coming out of this particular valley. This young man had come to the end of a hard fight, and was about to be killed; however, as he chose to rise and fight again instead of giving up, he said that it was just the beginning of who he was and not the end. Of course, the idea is that when the devil tries to defeat us, he does not bring us to our end, but rather he brings us to our beginning. He is used by God to make us stronger, aware of our abilities, and more dependent on our God. What a powerful truth this is! God prepares us for our destiny if we choose to walk in it, and he is putting us through the fire not to destroy us but to make us ready. A lot of trust and faith in God is required to walk through that fire.

No doubt there have been many who attempt to reach their own destinies by sidestepping the fires, or once within the fire, they refuse to go all the way through. I learned that trusting the Lord and what he is doing in my life, even though I may not understand the reasons, helps me continue to walk forward. How we respond to life is what makes us different and sets us apart. We can respond with choosing to persevere with our eyes on the Lord, or we can respond with quitting or not even attempting great things. But no one is unique in walking through difficulties in life. All of us will have those. We just need to choose to not try to maintain control over life and admit that God already is in control. Our choice rests in how we respond to life and what God allows in it. Do we trust God, or with much frustration, do we attempt to be the ones in control?

I was once silenced, silenced by the enemy. That was his attempt at defeating me. I was afraid to be who God had created me to be and to walk into my own part of his story. I allowed the fear of man to keep me silent, and I even allowed the fear of my parents to keep me quiet about my opinions and beliefs. I struggled with my confidence and with my identity, and I unexpectedly ran into depression and anxiety issues. All were attempts by the enemy to destroy me and defeat me. But God had chosen me to be a voice for him, a voice to teach his Word boldly and to encourage others to walk forward in their own destinies. It is time for me to rise up from this fight, nearly defeated and about to give in. This is only the beginning of who I am and who I will continue to become and not my end. Join me in this new adventure of being silenced no more.

Epilogue

I feel as though I have left some of my story open-ended and wish to share more. In a most respectful way and in a timing led by the Lord, I shared with my mother my emotions about how I felt when she mistreated me. I also outlined my stance about how I needed boundaries between us. Being heard by her and conquering the fear that held me back from this honesty truly brought great healing to my heart. She may never change in this lifetime, but I know that I have.

Being eager to please the Lord instead of man, my husband and I continued to pray for direction from God and asked him to lead us to the right church after our return from overseas. After downloading an East Asian Bible app, my husband accidentally came across a church website that we had not heard about. He became interested in visiting that specific church and shared this with me. At first, I did not know if that was the answer for us, but after asking the Spirit to be very clear with us about where to go, I decided to listen to a sermon on spiritual gifts off that church's website. My husband and I both listened to the teaching and felt an excitement that this could be our new church home. The next morning we went to visit this church, and after the service the lead pastor took time to meet us, share with us the vision of the church, and answer a whole bunch of questions that my husband and I had for him. After that conversation my husband and I realized that this was the church body we were looking for, a church open to the supernatural and yet firmly rooted in the Word.

The Lord spoke into my spirit that he was doing a new thing in the church today. American churches have been torn and divided because of theology differences and strong doctrinal stances. This oftentimes feels like a civil war. Many are taught to embrace a conservative teaching where the power of God in miracles and wonders no longer exist in today's church. And on the other hand, there are believers who only seek what God can give them and neglect to be rooted in his Word and live out their faith in obedience. Neither group has received a revelation of who God is. If they did, they would discover that God continues to work in power today and that he desires for us to seek him out rather than what he can do for us. Sure, God blesses his children and responds to our prayers, but if our motivations are selfish, then that is evidence of a lack of discipleship. For me and my husband, we felt caught within the trenches of this war, and like so many, we became victims of the damage that had taken place. But out of these trenches covered in dirt and blood, we chose to hope that these divisions will not be an issue in the near future. We have recognized that the side we were once on was in fact the side that was hurting me. We have chosen to cross the battlegrounds and join a new side that we feel pleases God the most. He is making his children hungry for more of him and thirsty for righteousness, and the result is a body of believers being truly discipled. These believers are made free to believe that the power of God we see in the Bible is for his children today too. Jesus is the same yesterday, today, and tomorrow.

I have also started a ministry this previous spring that God placed in my heart during the last year of service overseas. I have enjoyed this new ride of faith with much expectation of what he will do with the unlimited creative vision he has blessed me with. The joy of walking in this new freedom has brought more hope into my life that I delightfully embrace every day. Loving life and loving what I do for the Lord has been a pursuit of mine for a great length of time. Will you join me in this venture to see what God has destined for you with all the uniqueness that you are? Will you join me in believing that God has the best in mind for you? I know he is waiting for you to step out and embark on an adventurous journey that he paved for you since before he created you!

About the Author

Tabitha Crusoe has spent over six years in service as an overseas missionary alongside her husband Jordan, where their focus was planting churches, sharing the gospel, and pursuing discipling new believers. Although they are currently living stateside they have a desire to return back overseas again in the future. Tabitha has studied Bible in college and has a passion to teach God's Word to international audiences as well as women living in the States.

Printed in the United States
By Bookmasters